# *THE MARKET-PLANNED ECONOMY OF YUGOSLAVIA*

by SVETOZAR PEJOVICH

*University of Minnesota Press, Minneapolis*

Printed in the United States of America at the
North Central Publishing Company, St. Paul

Library of Congress Catalog Card Number: 66-18868

PUBLISHED IN GREAT BRITAIN, INDIA, AND PAKISTAN BY THE OXFORD
UNIVERSITY PRESS, LONDON, BOMBAY, AND KARACHI, AND IN CANADA
BY THE COPP CLARK PUBLISHING CO. LIMITED, TORONTO

*to the memory of Joseph Schumpeter*

# PREFACE

SINCE the end of the Second World War, research efforts in the economics of socialism have been directed largely toward bettering knowledge and understanding of the Soviet economy. This was, of course, a reasonable consequence of the overall postwar international development which made the U.S.S.R. our most formidable ideological adversary and also the largest socialist state. However, the fact that the Soviet economy has been characterized by a predominance of administrative-command relations between the government and productive units has precluded our following a brilliant pioneering work of Oskar Lange and Fred M. Taylor, *On the Economic Theory of Socialism* (University of Minnesota Press, 1938) and, consequently, from constructing a general economic theory of socialism. This emphasis on the Soviet economy per se directed our attention from the theoretical and toward the institutional approach, with the result that the majority of available texts – and, therefore, courses – in comparative economic systems are more descriptive than analytical. (Two notable texts that are exceptions would be W. G. Nutter's *The Growth of Industrial Production in the Soviet Union* (Princeton University Press, 1962) and Branko Horvat's *A Theory of Economic Planning* (Belgrade: Yugoslav Institute for Economic Research, 1964).)

On the basis of the latest developments within the socialist bloc, where pressures to substitute economic relations for administrative-command relations seem to be mounting, it has become increasingly clear that socialism is not the Russian monopoly of today and that there is a pressing need for the economic profession to restore its emphasis on the theoretical approach begun with Lange, and pay more attention to the working of economic laws within the socialist framework – whatever it might be at a given time. In order to be able to measure, assess, explain, understand,

and even predict the economic performance of socialist states, we need to build a valid core of economic theory of socialism.

This study is a step in this direction, though at least some descriptive material could not be avoided. But the main purpose of the study is to provide a strong analytical content so that this work can be considered as a test (and a supplement, because of its emphasis on dynamic economics) of the Lange theoretical framework of a socialist economy, relying heavily on economic planning through a relatively free market. For this reason, the analytical-descriptive format of the study is not too closely tied to current data and is, in fact, relatively independent of them. The reader will become aware of this when reading Chapter V, in which Schumpeter's theory of economic development is offered as the best basis for understanding the performance of the Yugoslav economic system, and, consequently, of a decentralized socialist economy.

I chose the Yugoslav economic system as the source of my generalizations because I attempt in this work to abandon the institutional approach to the problems of the economics of socialism and to answer the question whether one can formulate an economic theory of socialism and demonstrate to the socialist leaders, among others, that a decentralized socialist state can *control* both the level of economic activity and the allocation of resources – and, consequently, the composition of output – at least as efficiently as can the administrative-command economy of the Soviet type. For this reason the reader familiar with the structure of the Yugoslav economy may criticize the book for failing to elaborate on the importance of some institutions in Yugoslavia such as communes, trade unions, self-governing Chambers and associations, and so forth. Well aware of this omission, I ask the reader to recall, whenever he raises this type of objection, that the primary purpose of this book is to use the Yugoslav experience to provide an additional step in formulating the general economic theory of socialism.

The Yugoslav economic system has been selected for a number of reasons. One is the uniqueness of the Yugoslav economy. Yugoslavia is the first East European country which has *actually* decentralized its economic system without giving up economic planning from the center.

In addition to what might be called a growing conversational consensus among social scientists, there are some indications that the socioeconomic evolution taking place in the U.S.S.R. will lead that country toward a more decentralized economic system. For example, in *Pravda* on August

17, 1964, a Soviet academician advocated "a system of bonuses, taxes, fines, and flexible prices and greater leeway for decision making by plant managers instead of detailed planning and supervision by central planning authorities" (quoted by Theodore Shabad in his article "Profit-Plan Talk Revived in Soviet" (New York *Times*, August 18, 1964, p. 8)). Also, at the end of September 1964, Premier Khrushchev announced that "the production of consumer goods must be given 'first priority' in a new long-range economic development plan to be drafted for the Soviet Union" (quoted by Shabad in "Khrushchev Urges 'First Place' for Output of Consumer Output" (New York *Times*, October 2, 1964, p. 10)).

This shift in resources from heavy to light industry would call for the analysis of the structure of aggregate demand, i.e., the structure of individual wants in the U.S.S.R., and would, in turn, cry for some use of market mechanism. And in 1965 the leaders of the U.S.S.R. and many other East European countries set in motion – perhaps reluctantly, but definitely – a number of economic and organizational innovations leading toward a greater degree of freedom of the basic production units from their respective centers. Thus, this book should be valuable for teachers of courses in the Soviet economy, since it significantly compares some definite trends of the kind now present in the U.S.S.R. and forecasts their possible future. This fact that the Yugoslav economic system can be used for comparisons with and for forecasts of the U.S.S.R. system greatly increases its worldwide importance.

The Yugoslav economic system has already had a profound influence on newly emerging countries in Africa and Asia. The basic principles of economic planning in India are similar to those in Yugoslavia, and the distribution of profits of enterprises in the U.A.R. reflects the procedure applied in Yugoslavia since 1953. The *Journal of Commerce*, in a long article on Yugoslavia in March 1962, said that "Yugoslavia's experience might become some kind of model for underdeveloped nations," and the editors of the New York *Times* wrote on March 27, 1962, that "more detached observers may understand that in such difficult, unprecedented experimentation some mistakes are natural and lessons must be learned. The Yugoslav troubles pale into insignificance by comparison with the distress and hunger produced by the kind of economic planning practices in Russia under Stalin and in China."

All of which leads to this conclusion: the Yugoslav economic system is unique. It contains characteristics of both a centrally planned and a free-market economy, and its emergence therefore represents a major innovation in the economics of socialism.

To cut down on interruptions of the analysis in the text, it seems advisable to make a few important points here.

In 1918, the Kingdom of Serbs, Croats, and Slovenes, later renamed Yugoslavia, was created. The emergence of this multinational state was the final expression of the long-cherished dream of the southern Slavs. However, as often happens to romantic dreams and ideas, a large number of grave problems arose almost immediately after the creation of the kingdom. These problems had their common origin in the fact that the cultural, political, and economic history of the Serbs on the one hand, and the Croats and Slovenes on the other, had proceeded along completely different paths. The Serbs, dominated by the Turks for about five hundred years, found themselves economically inferior to the Croats and Slovenes, whose social and economic development had flourished under Austrian rule. For example, in 1918, three-fourths (74.73 per cent) of 1,855 existing manufacturing enterprises were located in the former Austrian provinces according to S. Kukoleca (*Industrija Jugoslavije* (Belgrade: Balkanska Stampa, 1941)).

As a result, the Croats and Slovenes considered themselves superior to the Serbs, and the Serbs, in turn, believed that they had liberated the rest of the country from the Austrian rule and should therefore have political supremacy over the Croats and Slovenes.

The fundamental change in the socioeconomic system after the Second World War has not, so far as one can judge from a distance, solved the problem of political chauvinism and rivalry in Yugoslavia. Occasional criticism of this chauvinism by the Yugoslav press and, in particular, a few of Tito's speeches in 1964 and 1965 testify that the problem is still very much alive indeed. That the cultural and economic gap between different national groups in Yugoslavia has not yet been bridged is evident from the figures in Chapter III.

In fact, the shift of the early 1950's from administrative planning to a more decentralized economy heavily relying on the market mechanism irritated provincial chauvinism. A logical consequence of the introduction of market criteria into the economic system was the tendency for investment funds to move into more developed areas. To offset the negative political repercussions of this tendency, the Yugoslav government continued to finance investment projects in less developed areas through the budget, as the reader can see from the budget data for 1963 in Chapter I.

"Local government" will frequently be referred to in the text of this book. The reader will realize that sweeping economic reforms since the early 1950's could not leave the structure of the three levels of government (federal, republic, and local) untouched – in fact, political and economic changes proceeded hand in hand. For this reason, the world-wide significance of the Yugoslav experiment would call for a study of the political structure of the country. However, in this book I shall ignore the organizational structure of the local government. Whatever its organization may be, it is an organ of state, and as such it performs a number of social, economic, and political functions for the area under its jurisdiction. The reader can find an extensive analysis of the organization and duties of the local government (commune) in the U.N.E.S.C.O.'s *International Social Science Journal*, Vol. XIII, No. 3 (1961), pp. 379–457. As far as this book is concerned, it suffices to remember that the decentralization of the economy made necessary increased relative independence of local governments. One major task of the local government is to increase the economic base within its territory and raise the standard of living. More will be said about the revenue of the local government later in the text. There were eight hundred local governments in 1960, with an average population of about 22,500. There is a strong tendency for greater numbers of citizens to participate in the work of local governments. The number was 68,933 in 1960, but the reader should be aware that the communes are more often than not dominated by a few party members.

The Yugoslav economy distinguishes between "fixed" capital – i.e., capital invested in machinery, buildings, and means of transportation – and "circulating" capital – i.e., capital invested in raw materials, inventories, unfinished products, tools of less than three years' durability, and cash.

The Yugoslav unit of currency is the dinar. In January 1961 the International Monetary Fund and the Yugoslav government agreed to establish an exchange rate of 750 dinars for one United States dollar, and on July 25, 1965, a new exchange rate of 1,250 dinars for one United States dollar was announced.

Yugoslavia is a federal state consisting of six "Socialist Republics" – Bosnia and Herzegovina, Croatia, Macedonia, Montenegro, Serbia, and Slovenia.

American aid has been an important factor in the development of the Yugoslav economy since 1949. Considerations of preserving the newly won Yugoslav independence from the Soviet Union determined the nature and size of American aid. There can be no question but that American aid and aid from other Western countries had positive effects on the rate of economic growth in Yugoslavia – providing the Yugoslav economy with food, capital goods, and extensive technical assistance and encouraging the evolving economic decentralization (initiated in principle in June 1950, and established in 1953) because of the psychological and political side-effects produced by prompt and ample Western aid in a period of grave crisis.

In preparing this manuscript for publication I received substantial support and encouragement from a number of my friends. I should like to thank them all for their unselfish help.

My greatest gratitude goes to Professor Cyril Zebot of Georgetown University, who actively participated in the work on this book. His intellectual drive, academic standards, and warm friendship are virtually built into its foundation. The final draft of the manuscript reflects the contribution of Mr. Joseph Shechtman, then of the University of Minnesota Press. Mr. Shechtman went far beyond the call of duty in encouraging me to prepare the manuscript for publication and following my work very closely and critically step by step.

Professor O. H. Brownlee made an important, and to him probably unknown, contribution to this book. During my stay at the University of Minnesota as a Ford Foundation Fellow, he convinced me of the relation between a successful and rewarding academic career and creative research. I am also grateful to my colleague at St. Mary's College, Brother K. Basil, for his intellectual encouragement and support.

The financial assistance of the Earhart Foundation in preparing the first draft of this book and the Relm Foundation grant to the University of Minnesota Press in support of its publication are gratefully acknowledged, as is the permission from Georgetown University to use material from my doctoral thesis.

Svetozar Pejovich
*Associate Professor, University of Dallas*

*February 12, 1966*
*Winona, Minnesota*

# *TABLE OF CONTENTS*

# THE MARKET-PLANNED ECONOMY OF YUGOSLAVIA

# I THE LEGAL STRUCTURE OF THE YUGOSLAV ECONOMY

THE transformation of the Yugoslav economy after the Second World War is reflected in the pattern of change in its organizational framework. The legal acts discussed in this chapter have been chosen for a comprehensive picture of these changes; they show that the Yugoslav economic system has undergone unusually frequent and substantial organizational overhauling since 1945. The economic significance of these changes will be analyzed in later chapters in this study.

The laws and regulations noted in this chapter reveal three basic organizational innovations in the Yugoslav economy. The first was engendered by the Law on the Economic Plan of 1946. This act stated the general principles of the organizational structure of the Yugoslav economy. It also indicated the course to be followed by subsequent legal provisions for coping with contemporary problems. The main characteristic of the Yugoslav economic structure as determined by the Law on the Economic Plan of 1946 was a complete subordination of economic criteria (demand, supply, price-output decisions, etc.) to administrative-command relations.

The second organizational innovation was triggered by two legal acts: the Law on Management of Government Commercial Enterprises by Workers' Collectives of July 1950, and the Law on Planned Management of the National Economy of December 1951. This innovation marked the beginning of the replacement of administrative-command relations by economic ones in Yugoslavia. It took some time for the legislature to decide how to deal with the problems which were bound to appear as soon as the administrative-command regulations were softened and the system of incentives by sheer compulsion was abandoned. In fact, the changeover occurred in agriculture in 1954, in the allocation of investment funds in 1954, in the handling of capital goods in December 1953, in income distribution within enterprises in December 1953, in the liquidation of unprofitable enterprises in December 1953, in the banking system in 1954–56, and in the price system in 1954 and 1955 when price-fixing agreements among enterprises were forbidden.

These turning points demonstrate an interesting time lag. The problems which were bound to arise almost immediately after the principles were stated in the period 1950–51 were not explicitly and precisely regulated until December 1953. And then it took the government three full years to cope with them. It was only toward the end of 1956 that the principles enunciated in the period 1950–51 were fully implemented. The main features of the Yugoslav economy in the years following 1957 were, first, the increased scope of economic criteria in the organization of production and distribution, and, second, the rising power of the banking system. The government, however, maintained its control over the economy through a number of economic and political devices such as the basic propositions of the Social Plan (to be discussed below) and the supervision of enterprises by the banking system and local governments.

The third reorganization of the structure of the Yugoslav economy started at the end of 1962, continued throughout the early 1960's, and reached its climax in the summer of 1965 when a number of comprehensive economic reforms were announced. The indications are that the major aim of those reforms is to enlarge the independence of enterprises from administrative control, and to strengthen the role and importance of the market mechanism.

### ACQUISITION OF PROPERTY RIGHTS BY THE STATE

There were in Yugoslavia three legal means for the acquisition of property rights by the state: nationalization of private property, confiscation, and expropriation. *Nationalization* is the transfer of well-defined property rights from individuals and/or private groups to the state. The act of nationalization is impersonal and indiscriminate, pertaining to all holders of well-defined property rights. The dispossessed owners are usually entitled to receive compensation determined either by the state or by the prevailing market price. *Confiscation* of property arises in the transfer to the state of well-defined property rights from a person found guilty in the courts of crimes so punishable. There is, of course, no compensation for confiscated property. *Expropriation* is the transfer of property rights in real estate from individuals to the state when such transfer is, in the opinion of the state, in the social interest (e.g., expropriation of land from peasants to build railroads). Expropriation can be appealed to a court, whereas nationalization and confiscation cannot.

The government of Yugoslavia has employed all three of these means in its postwar economic policies.

The Law on Confiscation of Private Property was enacted on June 12, 1945,[1] and supplemented by the Law on Confiscation of July 13, 1946.[2] These laws empowered courts to order confiscation of the private property of persons found guilty of crimes punishable, according to the law, by confiscation. These laws also specified the property to be excluded from the confiscation in order to provide for the minimum support needed by the family of the convicted criminal.

The Law on Expropriation was enacted on April 4, 1947,[3] and more elaborate directions for its implementation were announced on September 6, 1948.[4] The purpose of this law was to furnish the state with the legal basis for acquisition of property rights in the social interest. The law provided that the act of expropriation can be issued by the Federal Government, governments of the People's Republics, local governments, and the Ministry of Defense. The act of expropriation must contain (1) the name of the government agency issuing the order, (2) the purpose of the expropriation, and (3) the amount and the terms of payment to the dispossessed owner. The amount of compensatory payment is to be determined according to the prevailing market price.

Both the Law on Confiscation and the Law on Expropriation have been, since 1945, the government's measures against individuals and private groups who were considered hostile to the existing order or who possessed real estate at places marked for some future public use. The 1946 Law on Nationalization[5] of private enterprises, on the other hand, meant the transfer of well-defined ownership rights from all individuals and private groups to the state. The law included industrial enterprises, mines, transport facilities, banks, wholesale trade, and foreign commercial enterprises. The second (1948) Law on Nationalization[6] included retail trade and catering establishments. The third Law on Nationalization[7] was enacted on December 31, 1958. This law amended the legislation on nationalization to include all private apartment buildings and houses having in excess of two large or three small apartments.

The only survivors of the laws for the nationalization of private businesses have been artisans, who still have their own private shops. Their operations were first regulated by the Law on Handicrafts of June 6, 1949.[8] The provisions of this law were very loose and left a significant margin of discretion to local governments. The crucial provision concerning new entry is a good example of the incompleteness of the law. The legal requirements which an applicant had to meet in order to receive a permit to open his own shop were stated, but the law did not require local governments to issue permits to those who qualified; they could reject any qualified applicant at their discretion. The law had significance only to the extent that no person without skill could receive a permit to open a shop. The Law on Handicrafts of January 29, 1954,[9] which superseded the 1949 law, was far more precise. The new law established three crucial regulations: (1) shop owners may employ a maximum of five hired workers, (2) shop owners have to pay a special tax on "hired labor" (this tax has its origin in a dogmatic interpretation of the Marxist concept of surplus value), (3) the requirements which a potential shop owner has to meet in order to qualify for a permit are set forth: (a) the applicant must have a certificate of skill, (b) he must be a citizen of Yugoslavia, (c) he must be under no restriction (imposed exclusively by courts for well-defined crimes) against engaging in the particular trade. Once these requirements are met the local government must issue a permit to the applicant.

The laws on nationalization supplemented by the laws on confiscation and expropriation gave the Yugoslav government full control over industry and trade. Besides artisans only farmers and attorneys-at-law are private entrepreneurs in Yugoslavia. The policy of the Yugoslav government to date has been to encourage lawyers to extend their private practice and to encourage artisans and private farmers to join so-called cooperatives. However, no administrative pressure has been exerted to drive artisans and farmers into cooperatives. The means usually employed by the government have been primarily of a financial nature, such as the imposition of high taxes and restrictions of the credit available to private artisans and farmers.

Discrimination has been especially aimed against farmers; this is readily apparent when we compare the income tax scales imposed on farmers, artisans, and attorneys. On an income of 250,000 dinars, which is comparable to a factory wage, a farmer pays a tax of 45,000 dinars, an artisan 34,000 dinars, and an attorney 37,500 dinars. On an income of 700,000 dinars, the farmer would pay 210,000, the artisan 145,000, and the attorney 105,000.[10]

## YUGOSLAV AGRICULTURE

The analysis of Yugoslav agriculture must be developed against the background of two important factors: (1) prewar Yugoslavia was predominantly an agrarian country, with approximately three-fourths of the labor force employed in agriculture,[11] and (2) historical experience indicates that every communist government is hostile to private farmers. This is not exactly a Marxian proposition, for Marx thought that farmers would disappear as a major social class before the advent of socialism.

The analysis of the agricultural policies of the Yugoslav government after 1945 will be divided into three sections: agrarian reforms, peasants' cooperatives, and the government's credit policy.

*Agrarian Reforms in Yugoslavia after 1945.* There have been two agrarian reforms in Yugoslavia since 1945. The first was announced shortly after the war, on August 28, 1945.[12] According to this reform, land was taken away from (1) nonfarmers who possessed land in excess of 30 hectares (a hectare is 2.471 acres); (2) churches and monasteries in excess of 10 hectares; (3) peasants in excess of 30 hectares per family; (4) nonfarmers (who possessed less than 30 hectares) in excess of 5 hectares. The state used the land acquired by this reform for creating state farms, and for rewarding with 8 to 12 hectares of land those families who sided with Marshal Tito's Partisans during the war and who had no land. The second agricultural reform was announced on May 27, 1953.[13] It set 10 hectares of arable land (24.71 acres) as the maximum of land per family; everything over this was taken from each family that possessed this excessive amount of land and distributed among the state farms and the farmers' working cooperatives. The government paid between 30,000 and 100,000 dinars per hectare to the original owners, according to the arability of the land which was nationalized.

This second agrarian reform can be called the forced reform. Two months earlier, on March 30, 1953, the Yugoslav government had given up its drive to compel the collectivization of the peasants. Moreover, those peasants who had already been collectivized were permitted to leave the cooperatives, taking their property with them. The majority of peasants left the cooperatives and those who decided to stay were, for the most part, the poorest peasants, those who could not expect anything better from leaving their cooperatives. As a consequence, the farmers' working cooperatives became a heavy financial burden to the state. The state found that it had to make a choice: to liquidate these cooperatives or to enact another agrarian reform and provide the farmers' working cooperatives with sufficient land. The government chose the agrarian reform as the way out.

The two agrarian reforms were probably the two least resisted major economic measures among those undertaken by the government after 1945. The explanation is to be found in the fact that the average amount of land per farm in prewar Yugoslavia was a little over five hectares and that 88.3 per cent of all farms had less than 10 hectares, that is, less than 24.71 acres.[14]

*Cooperatives.* It is an observable fact that a communist government tends to collectivize farmers. A number of reasons can explain this tendency. One is the assumption that a better division of labor can be achieved in the cooperative, and another is the assertion that collectivization of peasants would "liberate" surplus labor for factory work. However, it is quite possible that the main reason for this drive to put farmers into collectives is political rather than economic.

The first Law on Cooperatives in postwar Yugoslavia was enacted on July 23, 1946.[15] This law said that membership in cooperatives is voluntary, that one is free to leave the cooperative at will taking along his property, and that cooperatives are established by those who see their interest in them, i.e., by the peasants themselves, who have to submit their application to the local government for permission to form a cooperative. The law gave the state a double control over the activities of cooperatives. First, the State Commission for Cooperatives was to control the economic activities of cooperatives to assure the government that they were in agreement with the overall economic plan, and second, local governments were given direct political control over cooperatives in their territory.

On June 9, 1949, the Law on Farmers' Cooperatives[16] was enacted, marking the beginning of the drive of the Yugoslav farmers into collectives. This law did not make collectivization compulsory. On the contrary, leaving it up to the farmers to decide whether they wished to join a cooperative and what type of cooperative life they would prefer if they decided to collectivize, it provided for a variety of types of collectivism. It was left to other legal means to induce farmers to join a particular type of cooperative.

The law made three general statements about all types of collectives. (1) The property of a cooperative comes from three different sources: property supplied by the state, property brought in by the members, and property accumulated in the course of time. (2) Every cooperative has to work out an economic plan and have it approved by the local government. The approval of the plan by the local government makes it a part of the overall economic plan. (3) The ruling bodies of a cooperative are (in order of their importance) the assembly of all members, the executive board, and the supervisory board. The latter two are to be elected by and from the members of each cooperative.

The Law on Farmers' Cooperatives provided for two basic types of associations of farmers. One was *agricultural cooperatives*. Farmers who decide to join an agricultural cooperative keep their own property. Their income is derived from what they have grown on their land. They may be asked to lend their tools to the other members of the cooperative, or they may borrow tools they need from the cooperative. In each case, the law said, rent has to be paid to the owners of the tools. The cooperative benefits its members by providing better and/or cheaper seeds, by improving marketing (trucks, for example, would not pay an individual farmer but become profitable when farmers organize), and by furnishing other services.

This type of cooperative life has been known among the Slavs for centuries. They call it *zadruga*. V. Jagich, a Croatian historian and philologist, wrote in 1867:

> Long and patient investigation of the work done by modern historians such as Shifaric, Dumler, Hilferding, and F. Racki has shed more light on the past of our people from ancient times up to now. There are still a number of surviving customs which are so characteristic of our people as part of the Slavic group that it is impossible even today to recognize what is our old oneness and what customs developed later on. In the first place should be mentioned the cooperative life that has lasted up to these days and which was, no doubt, brought in by Croats and Serbs from the north.[17]

In Slovenia, for example, the entire agricultural economy before the Second World War was organized in a network of such cooperatives. A well-known American writer said that "the people of Slovenia had achieved a near Utopia of cooperative social and economic life, before the Nazi terror struck."[18] This is the type of cooperative life which the

Yugoslav farmers would not object to at all. It represents — as worded in the law — the codification of a long tradition.

The law called the second type of cooperative the *farmers' working cooperatives.* This type is similar to the Soviet kolkhoz. The farmer has to turn in his property, and he receives payments for his work from the total product of the cooperative regardless of his subscribing property share. The law of 1949 provided for three varieties of farmers' working cooperatives. First, farmers could agree to retain ownership rights to property they turned in when they joined the cooperative (but not the use of the property, of course) and to receive payments of rent from the cooperative in addition to the regular payments for their work. Second, they could agree to retain ownership rights but to give up rent. Finally, they could agree to transfer their property altogether to the cooperative. In any case, the law allowed farmers to retain, if and when they decided to join a farmers' working cooperative, one hectare of arable land and their house. Farmers could leave their cooperatives only after three years from the day they joined. They could take their property along with them unless, of course, they had decided when they joined to transfer their property rights to the cooperative.

The Yugoslav government preferred farmers to organize into farmers' working cooperatives rather than into agricultural cooperatives. The government employed various means to induce the farmers to join the farmers' working cooperatives. The Law on Income Tax of November 20, 1945,[19] though passed before the cooperatives were started, contained provisions that could be used as pressure. This law imposed taxes on farmers not on the basis of the value of their yearly product but according to what their local governments expected them to produce. This discretionary right of the local governments to judge the expected production of each farmer left the door wide open for overtaxation of "stubborn" farmers. Article 26 of the Law on Income Tax of August 21, 1948,[20] stated that "the rate of taxation should be such as to foster farmers' working cooperatives by means of lower taxes."

This drive for forced collectivization failed completely and on March 30, 1953, the Law on Reorganization of the Farmers' Working Cooperatives[21] was enacted. Farmers already collectivized were permitted to leave the cooperatives and their property rights were re-established so that they could take their property along with them. Furthermore, a new system of taxation was introduced whereby farmers had to be taxed according to the market value of their realized product. This principle of taxation, with sporadic modifications, has been maintained up to the present, and indications are that it will not be changed in the foreseeable future.

Several factors compelled the Yugoslav government to discontinue its drive toward compulsory collectivization. The rift with the U.S.S.R. was about to reach its peak. Foreign economic aid was becoming increasingly significant for the performance of the Yugoslav economy in those critical years. But the most important reason for the change in the government's agricultural policy was the resistance of the farmers themselves.

This stubborn resistance of the farmers to nationalization of their land was a striking contrast to the almost total lack of resistance by those whose factories, stores, banks, and apartment buildings were nationalized in 1946, 1948, and 1958. Why? It seems that this different behavior of farmers and capital owners may be explained by two facts: (1) Yugoslavia was basically a traditional peasant society. The farmers were defending more than economic property; they were defending their deeply rooted way of life. (2) The industrialists and merchants were a minority, and largely of foreign origin. They could not put up effective resistance.

*Credit in Agriculture*. The government credit policy in agriculture reflects the same trend observed in the laws on cooperatives. The Law on the Credit System of August 23, 1946 [22] provided for extending credit to cooperatives and their members but neglected to include independent farmers. Not until April 7, 1954, was the National Bank directed to set aside a fund from which amounts up to 100,000 dinars would be made available to independent farmers.[23] In comparison to the credits extended to the socialist sector of agriculture (state farms and cooperatives) the amount of money loaned out to the private farmers has been exceptionally small. In 1958, for example, "738 million dinars of short-term credits and 2,100 million dinars of long-term credits were granted to private peasants. In the same year agricultural enterprises and Peasant Work Cooperatives had short-term credits of 63 billion dinars and long-term credits of 42 billion dinars outstanding." [24] There were 2,618,103 private holdings in Yugoslavia in 1963 with a total area of 11,108,000 hectares and manpower of 5,585,000. The socialist sector in that same year consisted of 5,120 holdings with 2,430,000 hectares of land and manpower of 234,000.[25]

These data are evidence that a policy of discrimination against private peasants has been in force in Yugoslavia since 1945. However, one should not jump to conclusions about the extent of discrimination. Since private peasants cannot own more than 10 hectares of land per household they obviously cannot obtain substantial loans, their creditworthiness being low, and they could not possibly undertake such huge investments as irrigation projects and building modern stables.

## THE INSTRUMENTS CONTROLLING THE LEVEL AND DIRECTION OF ECONOMIC ACTIVITY

From the previous two sections of this chapter we have seen how the Yugoslav government accumulated in its hands the entire national wealth of Yugoslavia, except for that produced by private farmers and private artisans. This, of course, gave the government the opportunity, as well as the responsibility, of controlling the level and direction of economic activity. The instruments used by the Yugoslav government for maintaining economic activity at a high level and for channeling it in the direction preferred by the government will be described under four headings: the system of economic planning; the organization of the financial institutions; monetary policies; and fiscal policies.

*The System of Economic Planning.* On June 4, 1946, the Law on Economic Planning and Government Planning Agencies [26] was enacted. This law inaugurated the formal transformation of the Yugoslav economy from the prewar free-market economy to a centrally planned economy. The law said that the purpose of the economic plan was to guide the development of the national economy in the direction most favorable for the welfare of the people of Yugoslavia. The economic plan was prepared by the Federal Planning Commission, which was responsible directly to the Federal Government. Each of the six republics which constitute Yugoslavia had its own planning commission and so had every local government. The law followed rather closely the principles of economic planning in the U.S.S.R. No economic instruments were designated in this law concerning the relation between the state organs and enterprises and between the enterprises themselves. The Federal Planning Commission, together with the planning bodies in the republics and localities, was made responsible for allocation of supply, prescription of the quality of products, and determination of production quotas for each enterprise. An implication of this law was that, regardless of market conditions, each enterprise had to follow the administrative orders received from above. Furthermore, enterprises had to provide the Federal Planning Commission with data concerning their fulfillment of the plan and any other information the commission might decide to ask for. The Law on Economic Planning was a general law which indicated trends to be followed in the subsequent operational provisions.

The real meaning of the Law on Economic Planning of 1946 is clarified by the earlier Law Specifying Goods Subject to Planned Distribution and Consumption,[27] which subjected virtually all goods to planned distribution, and by the later Law on Imports and Distribution of Imported Goods,[28] according to which the import quota, along with the planned distribution of imported goods among enterprises and consumers, was to be determined by the Federal Planning Commission. The latter law prescribed the following process of import planning: each enterprise was to inform its direct superior, an administrative agency of the government, about materials it would need for the fulfillment of the plan. The enterprise also had to prove that the materials asked for were not produced in the country. The administrative agency considered import applications of all enterprises in its territory and domain of control and then submitted its proposal to the Federal Planning Commission, which, after consideration of all proposals from all administrative agencies, formulated the import plan for the country as a whole. The final consequence of the Law on Economic Planning was the enactment of the First Five Year Plan, 1947–51.

The Law on Economic Planning was abolished on December 30, 1951, when the Law on Planned Management of the National Economy was instituted.[29] The argument was that the failure of the old planning system had been due to the limits imposed by it upon the initiative of enterprises. To remedy this shortcoming the new law provided that, as of 1952, the parliament would adopt an annual Social Plan for the country as a whole, and might also enact long-range Social Plans for several years to come. The Social Plan should not, the law said, predetermine quotas, as the law of 1946 had done. The Social Plan sets the "basic proportions," leaving the quality and quantity of each product and its price to be determined by the producers themselves.

The constituents of the basic proportions are:

1. The minimum utilization of capacity in different industries for the

country as a whole and for individual republics — that is, the minimum expected aggregate supply.

2. The distribution of investment funds from the General Investment Fund (G.I.F.).*

3. The fund needed to meet payrolls at the level of minimum capacity utilization — that is, the aggregate wage bill or wage fund corresponding to the minimum expected aggregate supply.

4. The rate of accumulation by different branches of the economy.

5. The rate of social contributions and other payments by producers and their allocation to the G.I.F., the federal budget, and other budgets.

6. The determination of funds distributed through the federal budget.

Propositions 4–6 provide the means for executing the decisions about propositions 1–3.

The major qualitative difference between the two laws on economic planning is easy to grasp. The first one, which can be called the *production plan*, compelled enterprises to produce predetermined quotas of predetermined goods. The Social Plan, which can be called the *investment plan*, determines the allocation of the G.I.F. by branches of industry and geographical localities, leaving it up to the producers to determine the quantity and quality of their output, and also its price.

It is an old truth that there are basically two ways to maximize economic efficiency and the rate of development: compulsion and material incentives. Both rely on man's intellect and the power of his will to expand the scope of economic activity and to offset the working of the law of diminishing returns. The inducements used, however, are quite different. The Law on Economic Planning of 1946 rested on compulsion; the Law on Planned Management of the National Economy of 1951 indicated an increased scope for the system of incentives. I say "indicated" because this law did not introduce any concrete incentives into the economic system. Other provisions had to be made to establish the system of incentives for those who received money from the G.I.F. For this reason attention must be paid to the legal provisions which preceded and followed the Law on Planned Management.

*The G.I.F. is a sum of money whose size and origin is determined every year by the Social Plan. Sources of this fund are usually interest on capital paid by each enterprise, a percentage of the profit tax, etc. This fund is held at the National Bank, which must allocate it to all the specialized banks, which in turn distribute this money to the enterprises as loans. This fund should not be confused with bank credit, which comes from deposits and other revenue sources. In fact, the G.I.F. can be treated as autonomous investment.

The Law on Planned Management said nothing about the instruments to be used for the distribution of funds from the G.I.F. It took the government quite a while to remedy this shortcoming. On December 31, 1953, the first auction for investment loans from the G.I.F. was announced.[30] The act said that money from the G.I.F. would be auctioned when no other provision was made. When an auction is announced, those who are interested are invited to submit their applications. Such applications must state the purpose for which the loan is asked, the amount of the loan, the amount needed in foreign currency, the rate of interest the enterprise is willing to pay, the expected time for completion of the project, the amount of circulating capital as a percentage of total capital required for the project, and a fully elaborated investment project. During the period between the enactment of the Law on Planned Management and the Law on First Auction for Investment Loans the National Bank of Yugoslavia probably had the discretionary right to allocate free funds to enterprises of its own choice. I say this because between 1951 and 1954 the National Bank of Yugoslavia was *the* financial institution in the country responsible for channeling investment funds into physical projects, and voices were raised against the monopoly position of the bank.[31] The Law on First Auction introduced order into the procedure of allocation of funds, but did not erase the bank's monopoly position as the guardian and ultimate allocator of investment funds.

*The Financial System.* While the form and content of the Social Plan are discussed in the next chapter, the organization, rights, and duties of the agents responsible for the execution of the plan should be explained at this time. The organization of the Federal Planning Commission can be disregarded; whatever its organization it is an interpreter of the government's aims, which it has to translate into the basic propositions of the Social Plan. The distinctively economic activity starts when the plan is presented and the organs responsible for its execution start channeling investment funds into their different uses, and when direct producers start deciding what, how much, and of what quality to produce.

Before the Law on Planned Management was enacted the execution of the plan was accomplished through the budget. Every enterprise or group of enterprises producing the same or similar products had an administrative superior. The budget allocated investment funds to this administrative unit and its business was to transfer them to the enterprises under its control and to supervise their use. This system was abolished in 1952, and the distribution of investment funds was taken away from the budget and transferred to the banking system. At the same time the office of administrative superior was abolished and the bank and the enterprise were brought together.

The banking system in Yugoslavia has gone through three distinct phases. Until December 1953 the National Bank served as an intermediary whose task was to administer the financial plan, which was the monetary aspect of the overall economic plan. The second phase started in December 1953, when the first auction for investment loans was announced and the bank and the direct producer met to deal with each other without an intermediary administrative organ and without a definite, externally imposed obligation to come to a particular agreement. Once the relationship between the producer and the bank was "commercialized" a number of problems were bound to arise. Their clarifications and solutions required further adjustments in the banking system, and indeed its reorganization.

The Law on Banks and Postal Savings was enacted on January 28, 1954.[32] By this law communal banks were added to the banking system to help the National Bank in carrying out its responsibilities. The National Bank was required to execute the combined duties of a commercial bank, a central bank, and a bureau of the budget. As a commercial bank it collected deposits from private citizens and enterprises and extended credit to them. As the central bank it had to issue new money, control the balance of payments of the country, and publish statistics. As the bureau of the budget it was entrusted with control of the execution of the budget. The National Bank also had to perform other duties which the government would require of it. By law the revenues of the National Bank are accounted for under the following headings: commissions paid by the borrowers on approved loans, revenue from banking services, and other revenues. Its expenditures are salaries and wages paid to the employees of the bank, the costs of new issues of money, and other expenses. It is interesting to note that interest paid by the bank, as well as interest charged by the bank, is not considered as an expenditure or revenue of the bank. Any profit (or loss) in interest belongs to the federal budget.

The communal banks are established by the local governments.[33] The law provided that the National Bank should audit the books of the communal banks and that the latter must report to the former all their economic activities once a month. The revenue and expenditures of the communal banks are similar to those of the National Bank. The duties of the communal banks are those of commercial banks and the local bureaus of the budget. They collect savings and other funds of the enterprises in their territories, they control the execution of the local government's budget, and perform all other duties which the National Bank may transfer to them. There were 428 communal banks in 1961.[34]

The so-called specialized banks are assigned the duties of executing the credit and investment policy of the government.[35] The National Bank allocates funds to them from the G.I.F. and the specialized banks have to see that the most profitable projects are financed within the framework of the basic proportions of the Social Plan. The National Bank also allocates funds to the specialized banks to extend their own credits. These credits, which are separate from the money from the G.I.F., are also given on a competitive basis, but the banks have more freedom to move them from one use to another since they are not directly allocated by the plan. The specialized banks cannot control the process of production or the technology used but have both the right and the duty to see that funds are being used only for the projects and purposes for which the money was allocated.

The third phase began on March 15, 1961, when the Law on Banks[36] unified various legal provisions. The changes made by this law were significant only in an organizational way. The most important change concerned the function of the National Bank as a commercial bank. The National Bank of Yugoslavia no longer performs this function, which has been relegated to the communal banks and the three specialized banks. The National Bank, however, continues to perform the functions of a bureau of the budget and a central bank in addition to its important overall duty of allocating resources from the G.I.F. to the other banks and supervising their distribution to assure that there is agreement between the basic propositions of the Social Plan and the distribution of the G.I.F. among various industries.

*Monetary Policy*. Once the transition from the production plan of 1946 to the investment plan of 1951 was realized and the government controls over the level and direction of economic activity shifted from the realm of administrative-command relationships to the realm of primarily economic relations, monetary and fiscal policies became even more important. Under the conditions of the present system of investment planning the aim of government controls is to influence both the rate and pattern of investment. Some legal provisions which provide the operational framework for the allocation of funds from the G.I.F., and thus determine the way in which the monetary and fiscal policies are applied, will be considered first.

The Law on the First Auction (1953) was an early attempt to regulate the procedure of allocating investment funds directly to producers. The Law on Loans to Commercial Enterprises from the G.I.F. of January 28, 1954,[37] added another provision to those stated in the Law on the First Auction. It said that in deciding on an application for a loan the bank should take into consideration the applicant's financial status. Otherwise, this law confirms that funds from the G.I.F. should be distributed on a competitive basis. Further clarification of the distribution of investment loans was made in the Law on Investment Loans of July 25, 1956.[38] This law said that investment policy is to be carried out by the Yugoslav Investment Bank and other banks. Loans may be extended to commercial enterprises, banks, trade associations and other social organizations, farmers, and private artisans, and to private persons for homebuilding. Loans are to be given, according to this law, on a competitive basis, but enterprises may also submit applications even when no contest is being held. Loans may be for the enlargement of existing capacity, for new projects, for research, for the starting capital of new enterprises, and other purposes. This is an extremely important provision because the Social Plan merely allocates money to each industry, without specifying the ways funds can be used. The law, which confirmed the power of the banks over enterprises, ordered each prospective client to submit, together with the application for a loan, a statement specifying the purpose of the loan, the amount requested, the extent of internal financing (a new provision), the rate of interest the applicant is willing to pay, and setting forth the fully elaborated project. On February 6, 1957, the Law on Investment Loans was supplemented by the Law on the Cancellation of Contracts for Loans from the G.I.F.[39] The law excluded three industries from this provision: foodstuffs, building, and the electrical industry.

A careful reading of this law uncovers some interesting details. All industries producing consumption goods or capital goods for which there is a good market are excluded. The law also excludes borrowers who promise to produce for the market within eighteen months. Those who are not producing consumers' goods or goods for which there is strong demand or goods marketable in less than eighteen months will have their contracts revoked. This clearly affects only production of nonconsumption goods for which demand is weak. The extreme pro-market and pro-consumer significance of this act cannot be denied provided that it is agreed that income distribution in Yugoslavia is fair enough to be allowed to influence the allocation of the productive forces of the country. Whatever the government's investment decisions could have been earlier, the law changed them in favor of investments in *profitable* projects. Profits are, of course, always thought of in terms of expectations, i.e., they cannot be calculated in advance with the precision of mathematics. When a project is considered profitable this is only a subjective evaluation which may and often does prove incorrect. Hence, a heavy responsibility was put by this law on the allocator of investments funds—the banking system.

The rates of interest, with the exception of those offered by enterprises when competing for investment funds, are administered by the Federal Secretary of Finance. Usually the secretary determines the minimum and maximum rates of interest which can be charged or paid by the bank and leaves it up to the bank to vary its actual rate of interest within the legal bounds. The 1961 comprehensive regulation of the rate of interest[40] specifies the interest paid on individual savings (5 per cent), on funds deposited at the banks by enterprises (up to 7 per cent), on credits given by the National Bank to the specialized banks (up to 5 per cent), on credits extended to direct producers of goods and services (up to 10 per cent), and on loans extended by the specialized banks from the funds supplied to them by the National Bank (1 per cent above the interest the specialized banks pay to the National Bank). The rates of interest in the Yugoslav economy have been marked by a significant degree of rigidity, despite the fact that the Secretary of Finance can change them at his discretion. There is no reason to assume that the problem of time lag between the rise of a need to change interest rates and their actual change does not exist in Yugoslavia just as it does in all other countries.

But there was one far from rigid rate of interest in which the makers of Yugoslav economic policy had placed great hopes: the competitive rate of interest. It was believed in Yugoslavia from December 1953 until sometime in 1955 that the competitive rate of interest was the best possible device for the allocation of investment funds from the G.I.F. This is how it was supposed to operate. All enterprises in each industry were invited to compete for the fund of money available from the G.I.F. for that industry. In addition to the investment projects which they had to submit, they had to quote the rate of interest they would be willing to pay. The Yugoslav economists believed that higher interest rates offered should indicate higher prospective rates of return on investment. Once all applications were submitted, the amount of money required was determined by adding up the individual applications for loans. Given the supply and the demand schedules for funds in the industry the bank had to calculate and determine the marginal rate of interest at which all the money available would be invested.

The high expectations for the system in which the competitive rate of interest was the allocator of funds among competing users within the same industry (not between different industries since the elasticity of substitution of investment funds between different industries was close to zero because of the rigidity of planned proportions) turned to bitter disappointment. In order to get loans enterprises tended to offer higher rates of interest than they could reasonably afford, so that their applications had a better chance of being intramarginal. They hoped that the marginal rate would be lower than the one they offered; once the marginal rate was established all applicants paid only that rate. Since this behavior was more or less common to all enterprises the result was that the marginal rate of interest rose too high relative to the expected net returns. Finally, in March 1955, the government gave up the institution of competitive rates of interest as the primary instrument of investment fund allocation within each industry. In subsequent years its importance diminished further and in March 1961 the competitive rate of interest as an allocator of investment funds disappeared almost altogether.

This instrument having failed, on March 27, 1955, a new one was introduced: the guaranteed deposit.[41] The borrower, this act said, must deposit at the National Bank 5 to 10 per cent of the approved credit as a guarantee; this was refundable to him after the completion of the project.

The Law on Commercial Investment Loans of July 25, 1956, as we have seen, changed the whole procedure of allocation of funds by the banks once again. According to this law the borrower must assure the bank that he intends to participate in financing the project. This was in fact a change from the concept of a guaranteed deposit to the concept of obligatory internal financing. The aim of both requirements, guaranteed deposits and obligatory internal financing, was to decrease the excessive demand for credit.

An important change in the monetary tools which the government relied on in controlling the availability of loanable funds occurred in 1956 when the institution of reserve requirements, in the sense used in the West, was introduced into the economy. On July 18, 1956, the Law on Reserve Requirements of Banks at the National Bank was enacted.[42] According to this law the government had to set the range within which the National Bank, at its discretion, could vary the reserve requirements. The law set 50 per cent as the upper limit of the reserve requirement and instructed the National Bank to pay interest on amounts held as reserves. In its subsequent decision the National Bank set the reserve requirement at 30 per cent of the sum total of deposits held by the banks.[43] The Law on Reserve Requirements of Specialized Banks of April 5, 1961,[44] confirmed 30 per cent as the reserve requirement. The institution of reserve requirements indicates the rising importance of bank credits which are not channeled to the borrowers through some predetermined overall financial and economic plan; if they were, of course, there would be no need for reserve requirements.

The problem of price formation in Yugoslavia should be considered as a part of the monetary policy of the government. The ultimate effect of monetary policies as understood in the West is the control of the level of economic activity via changes in the supply of money. In a competitive economy a change in the money supply may affect the level of economic activity either by changing the volume of trade or by changing the price level or both. Moreover, a change in the price level affects income distribution and, ultimately, the composition of output. In Yugoslavia the government can change both the general price level and relative prices by its administrative decision. In this manner government policy with respect to the general price level becomes a form of monetary policy. The supply of money is adjusted to permit the execution of government policies, i.e., from being a cause of change in prices the quantity of money assumes the role of a permissive factor.

The problem of price formation in centrally planned socialist economies has long been a subject of controversy. There seem to be three schools of thought on this subject. The first group, represented by Von Mises and Hayek,[45] denies to the communist pricing system any rationality of its own. This school maintains that the saving device of the communist price system is the existence of market prices in the Western world. The second group, whose representative is Hirsch,[46] says that communist prices have a rationality of their own. This group maintains that a critical analysis of communist economies must deal primarily with the aims of those economies and judge their price systems only as to whether they are capable of bringing the aims into being. The third school of thought, represented by Lange, Dobb, and Sweezy,[47] considers Von Mises's and Hayek's thesis ill-taken. Price formation by professional experts, when based on full knowledge about the country's wealth and production capacities, on rigorous analysis of the most promising long-range objectives for the welfare of the people,* and on information about aggregate demand, in the opinion of this third group, should give better results than the trial-and-error price formation of a competitive economy. In fact, Lange thinks that planning processes are also based on trial and error, with the advantage that in a planned economy correction can be made more readily and with less cost; the planning board possesses better knowledge and can correct deficiencies as well as allow for changes in taste, shifts in demand, with less fluctuation of capital from one industry to another. He says: "The prices are 'planned' in so far as the preference scale is fixed by the Central Planning Board; but once the scale is fixed, they are quite determinate. Any price different from the equilibrium price would leave at the end of the accounting period a surplus or a shortage of the commodity in question and thus impair the smooth running of the production process. The use of the right accounting price is vital to avoid disturbances in the *physical* course of production and those prices are far from being arbitrary."[48]

He adds in a footnote and graph: "Let *DD* and *SS* be the demand and the supply curves respectively. *BQ* is the equilibrium price and *OB* the equilibrium quantity. If the price is set at *AP* the quantity *OA* is forthcoming while *OC* is demanded. As a result of the intervention of the Planning Board the quantity produced will be set somewhere between *OA* and *OC* [see Fig. 1]."[49]

Lange's argument is good but not altogether convincing. What we get from his argument and the diagram is that if the price is held at AP there could be no determinate price-output solution. There can be only a zone of determinateness.

*However, if the government says that improving the standard of living is a goal, then we must ask ourselves whether such an aim does not logically imply that people have to be free to direct production in accordance with their own needs and wants.

Prices had been fixed by the Yugoslav government early in 1945. The scarcity of supply due to war destruction justified price-fixing in the years following the war. However, the Law of the General Economic Plan of 1946 indicated that price-fixing by the government was more than a temporary measure. The First Five Year Plan set objectives to be attained, and the price system had to help to allocate resources along the lines needed for the fulfillment of the plan.

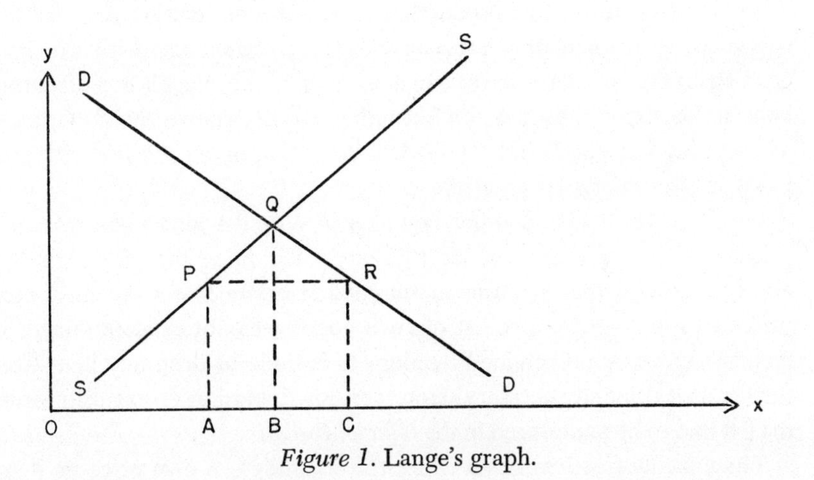


*Figure 1.* Lange's graph.

This policy was changed on January 17, 1951, when the Law on the Formation and Determination of the Prices of Consumption Goods was enacted.[50] This law was heralded by the government as a step in abolishing postwar rationing. In fact it was a step to abolish the institution of price-fixing. The law prescribed that retail prices, when no specific provision was made by law, should be determined in the following way: the price commission would decide average production costs of a given product from the reports of all enterprises engaged in its production. To this average cost the enterprises were allowed to add the rate of profit determined by the government for that particular industry. This law was reformulated on May 30, 1951,[51] when enterprises of local significance (those not engaged in what in the United States is called interstate commerce) were allowed to charge any price they found most profitable provided that the price was not below the average cost plus planned profit. On September 5, 1951,[52] the government changed this law for the third time in the same year. According to this reformulation all enterprises selling consumer goods were allowed to charge any price above the minimum, which still was the average cost plus planned profit.

These laws did not provide incentives to reduce average costs. In fact, they protected the established firms against entrants having lower costs. However, when these legal acts are considered in conjunction with the Law on Planned Management of the National Economy of 1951, which did away with production quotas, they manifest the introduction of forces other than administrative production quotas in determining price-output decisions; and when they are considered in connection with the laws on distribution of the total revenue of enterprises, which are discussed later in this chapter, the laws on formation and determination of the prices of consumption goods indicate a definite emphasis on the institution of profit as an optimizing criterion.

On June 18, 1952, another law was instituted which allowed enterprises selling consumers' goods to charge any price they found profitable,[53] although the government retained freedom to fix the maximum prices of some goods. The list of such goods was not predetermined; in fact, the government retained freedom to include or drop any item from the list as it deemed necessary. However, any inclusion or exclusion from the list had to be announced in the *Official Bulletin*.

The ensuing freedom of an enterprise to charge its own price on items not included in the list of price-controlled products led to a number of cartel-like agreements among enterprises producing the same or similar goods. The government's response was delayed and indeterminate. It enacted the Law on Wholesale and Retail Stores of August 17, 1955,[54] which forbade price-fixing and market-dividing agreements among enterprises engaged in buying or selling homogeneous or slightly heterogeneous products. However, the language of the law was very general, like the language of the antitrust laws in the United States.

As a result of the 1962 inflation the Law on the Social Control of Prices was enacted on July 25, 1962. An interesting feature of this law was an attempt by the government to retain its control over relative prices without at the same time falling back on strict administrative measures. The law stated that manufacturing enterprises retain their right to charge prices in accordance with the law of demand and supply, *but* that they must justify to the government authorities any proposed price increase. The government will in turn either approve or reject their action. Retail prices, on the other hand, should be calculated, the law said, on the basis of the price paid, plus transportation expenses, plus insurance premium, plus "planned" markup. Since the government agencies responsible for price control were to put special emphasis on maintaining price stability it follows that, although initial prices could have been market-determined, changes in consumers' preferences and income were not fully reflected in the corresponding changes of relative prices.

At the end of 1962 an impressive array of price categories existed in Yugoslavia. While the majority of prices were subject to the Law on Social Control of Prices, three more price categories existed in the country: for some goods, such as copper, aluminum, and oil, maximum prices were determined; for some others, such as electrical energy, transportation, and utilities, prices were fixed; and, finally, for most agricultural products minimum guaranteed prices were established.

This rather complicated price system led to both repressed inflation and misallocation of resources. To remedy this, the Yugoslav government announced on July 25, 1965, its decision to gradually abandon the system of administrative price control. The immediate effect of freeing some prices from the state control was an increase in the general price level by about 30 per cent.[55]

In summary, the Yugoslav price system is in part regulated by the government and in part administered by direct producers. It may be added that the farmers are completely free to charge for their products any price the market will bear. The government does not administer the farmers' selling prices, but it can and does influence them. After the harvest, wholesalers are in the market to buy wheat from the farmers. Farmers are not forced by law to sell their wheat, but the need for money for taxes and other expenses, as well as the problem of storage, will encourage them to sell. The wholesalers are not forced by law to buy all the wheat offered. The interaction of supply and demand in the market results in an equilibrium price. If that price is higher than the government wishes, the government can increase the supply by selling wheat from its reserves, thus forcing the equilibrium price down.

These prices that are regulated by the government are more than merely accounting prices. The government presumably knows from the market or from the producers the price which would be asked in the absence of controls. By fixing the price of a product above or below its potential market price the government affects the profitability of that particular branch of economic activity and, ultimately, the outcome of investment projects. In this manner, and at the price of misallocating resources, the Yugoslav government influences the composition of output and the direction of economic development by taking purely economic actions, without having to fall back on administrative-command relationships.

*Fiscal Policy.* As of December 1951, the federal budget ceased to be an instrument of primary importance for regulating the level of economic activity in Yugoslavia. Since then investment funds have been excluded from the budget. However, the Yugoslav budget still exercises an important effect on the national economy, serving as an instrument for reallocation of resources from the rich to the poor parts of the country. In 1963, it amounted to 15 per cent of the social product.

The major source of budgetary receipts is the turnover tax. It accounts for over 50 per cent of government revenue. The rationale of this tax was given by a Yugoslav economist in the following words: "This is an instrument used for regulating the market as well as for increasing or restricting the consumption of specific goods. . . . it ensures that the conditions of economic activity and the position of the enterprises in the market are made equal to a maximum degree." [56]

This turnover tax is one of the important features of the Yugoslav system taken from the Soviet Union; the question has often been asked why the Soviets (and the Yugoslavs, for that matter) do not introduce the easily administered progressive income tax. No attempt has been made to explain seriously and on theoretical grounds the reasons for the preference of socialist states for turnover taxation over progressive income taxation. A number of students have satisfied themselves by merely acknowledging the existence of turnover taxes. In 1955 Holzman published what is still the most comprehensive work on Soviet taxation. He asked the question, "Why do they prefer turnover taxes?" and noted three conceivable reasons: (1) the money illusion, i.e., Soviet citizens value the quantity of money more than its purchasing power; (2) if the labor supply curve in the U.S.S.R. is a rising function of money income, incentives to work will be strengthened by imposing indirect taxes instead of progressive income taxes; and (3) the marginal tax rates being higher than the average rates in the system of progressive taxation, the value of leisure relative to work tends to rise. Thus, it can be argued that regressive taxes have a less adverse effect on work incentives than progressive taxes because "Persons with low income have to pay high average rates of tax; the income effect induces them to work hard. Equally, persons with high incomes find that the cost of leisure rises with income, since the marginal rate of tax declines; this maintains their incentive to work."[57]

In summary, turnover taxes are expected to provide revenue without endangering the supply of labor, and to influence the composition of output. This explains the multitude of tax rates in Yugoslavia, ranging from zero to 40 per cent of the selling price, and also the almost constant changes in relative rates.

The taxation policy of the Yugoslav government goes far beyond the impact of turnover taxes. Various taxes paid by the Yugoslav firm enable the government to influence its investment behavior. The income taxes paid by farmers influence the supply of agricultural products in excess of farmers' domestic consumption. These two tax effects and especially the first one (the relationship between the taxation policy of the government and the investment behavior of the firm) are of far-reaching importance for the working of the economy as a whole and will be discussed more thoroughly in the following chapters. Table 1 presents the federal budget for 1963.

Table 1. The Yugoslav Federal Budget for 1963 (in Millions of Current Dinars)

| Receipts | | Expenditures | |
|---|---|---|---|
| Source | Amount | Purpose | Amount |
| Turnover tax | 398,467 | Investments financed through budget | 6,725 |
| Taxes paid by enterprises | 44,386 | Education | 194 |
| Receipts of the federal administration | 4,343 | Health and social security | 28,999 |
| Other receipts | 233,792 | National defense | 286,202 |
| Total[a] | 680,989 | Federal administration | 29,754 |
| | | Subsidies | 159,092 |
| | | Debt management | 32,964 |
| | | Other expenditures | 36,269 |
| | | Total[a] | 581,200 |

SOURCE: *Statisticki Godisnjak* (Belgrade: Savezni Zavod za Statistiku, 1964), pp. 268–269.

[a] Figures do not add up to totals.

## THE FIRM

This analysis of the legal framework has emphasized the path of transition of the Yugoslav economic system from the administrative-command economy to the semimarket economy. But the emergent economic criteria and the institution of profit, with their ever-increasing scope since 1950–

51, can be successful in practice only if the basic productive unit, the firm, is willing and able to respond. In other words, the system can work if and only if economic criteria have been substituted for the administrative criteria on the microeconomic level of the national economy. Since the whole of Chapter IV will be devoted to microeconomic considerations, the analysis here will confine itself to the general legal framework within which the Yugoslav firm operates.

*The Yugoslav Enterprise: Its Organization and Income Distribution.* On July 5, 1950, the Law on Management of Government Commercial Enterprises and Economic Associations by Workers' Collectives was enacted.[58] This law stated a few general principles about the workers' collectives without going into detail about their precise rights and duties. Taken by itself and divorced from the pattern of subsequent organizational changes, this law was a declaratory law with not much operational impact on the economy. It said that the workers' collectives (meaning all employees of an enterprise) conduct all activities of their respective enterprises through their managing organs, which are the Workers' Councils and Executive Boards. The Workers' Council of an enterprise has 15 to 120 members, depending on the size of the enterprise, and is elected by all the employees of the enterprise in a secret ballot. According to this law the duties of the Workers' Council consist of approving the production plan, suggesting changes in it, electing and dismissing the members of the Executive Board, establishing rules concerning discipline, lunch hours, and similar matters, administering the use of the net profit of the enterprise, and controlling the working conditions in the firm.

The Executive Board consists of 3 to 11 members, including the director. The members of the Board, except the director, are elected by the Workers' Council and have the following duties: preparing the production plan, preparing monthly operational plans, and seeing that the productivity of workers increases as much as possible.

To render this law operational the government had first to clarify the problem of handling the fixed capital of the enterprise, which up to that time was given to and taken from the enterprises by discretionary decisions of the government. The government also had to solve the problem of handling the revenue of the enterprises. Until 1950, the enterprise had simply to turn in its proceeds to the National Bank and get from it the funds allocated to the enterprise. Generally, the two had no correlation.

The first problem was solved by the Law on the Management of Fixed Capital by Enterprises of December 26, 1953.[59] This law gave the Workers' Councils the *right of use* over the fixed capital of the enterprise. The enterprise was given the right to sell its fixed capital, but not to a private person or a group of private persons. The right of use is acquired by producing capital goods, by buying them from others, and by getting capital goods from the government. Every loss caused by damage inflicted upon capital goods, the law provided, should be repaid to the government by the firm having the right of use. The enterprise also has to pay depreciation and interest on the book value of fixed capital.

Property rights under Yugoslav law are basically of two kinds. They are either absolute, due to all members of a society (*erga omnes*), or contractual, accruing only to the parties involved (*inter partes*). The right of use is an absolute right. The absolute rights are: (1) *ownership*, i.e., the right to use one's own property at will within the limits of law; (2) *jure in re aliena*, which can be (a) *the right of trespassing* (i.e., the right to cross another's land to reach, say, water), (b) *usus fructus* (i.e., the right to use a thing belonging to someone else or to rent it to others, but not to sell it or change its quality, or (c) *usus* (the right to use a thing belonging to someone else, but not to rent it or sell it or change its quality); and (3) *pawn*, the right to keep a thing but not to use it. To these legal institutions dating back to Roman law, which are accepted by all European continental countries, Yugoslav lawyers added still another absolute right: *the right of use*. This right has some similarities with *usus fructus* because the enterprise can use its means of production. It has some elements of *ownership* because the enterprise can sell them. But it is neither of the two. It is a wider right than *usus fructus* because the enterprise can sell its capital goods. It is a narrower right than *ownership* because the enterprise has to make payments for the use of its capital goods as a percentage of book value. When the enterprise sells its capital goods, it transfers to the buyer only the right of use. The government can, according to this legal institution, exercise its ownership rights only in case of liquidation of the enterprise. In such cases the government takes capital goods away before the procedure of satisfying unsettled claims starts.

The purpose of the right of use is dual: to safeguard the state's ownership over the capital goods of enterprises, and at the same time to increase economic efficiency in the allocation of means of production by allowing their free, i.e., unplanned, production and distribution among productive units.

As to the problem of income distribution, the Law on Distribution of Total Revenue of Enterprises of December 24, 1953,[60] ordered enterprises to distribute their incomes in the following manner (see Ch. IV for detailed analysis): (1) *material expenses* – raw materials, services, insurance, amortization; (2) *social contributions* – interest payments on the book value of fixed and circulating capital, turnover tax, rent (ground rent); (3) *rent on exceptional conditions* (location rent); (4) *payroll* – wages and salaries, contributions to social security; (5) *interest on short-term credits*; (6) *gross profit* (remainder after 1–5) – from which is taken tax on profit, tax on monopoly (when excessive profits are owing to a lack of competition), a percentage approved by the local government to the employees, a percentage to the local government; (7) *net profit* (remainder after 6) – Workers' Council decides whether it is to be used for expansion, for building apartments for workers, for scholarships, or for other projects, or whether it is to be kept in the bank as a reserve.

The Law on Distribution of Total Revenue of Commercial Enterprises of April 17, 1957,[61] introduced some changes into the system of revenue distribution by enterprises. The new pattern had this form: (1) *material expenses* – goods and services including 90 per cent of the advertising, services, and short-term credits; (2) *amortization*; (3) *social contributions* – interest payments on fixed and circulating capital, ground rent; (4) *turnover tax*; (5) *payroll*; (6) *gross profit* (remainder after 1–5) – from which is taken tax on profit; (7) *net profit* (remainder after 6) – Workers' Council distributes a percentage of it (up to one-half of net profit) to employees and a percentage to local government, makes an additional contribution for social security and communal buildings, and pays the rest into funds of the enterprise – reserve fund, collective consumption fund (scholarships, building workers' apartments, renting summer resort, etc.), and working capital fund (for reinvestment in fixed capital and in circulating capital).

Two important changes in the new law of 1957 may be noted. First, it includes in material expenses the cost of advertising. Beginning sometime in 1954, the role of advertising has been fast increasing. By 1957 a Yugoslav had only to turn on the radio, open any daily paper, or attend a soccer game in order to be exposed to extensive advertising for all kinds of products.

Another important change in the pattern of revenue distribution is related to the additional pay from profit. The law of 1957 allowed the Workers' Council to distribute up to one-half of the profit after taxes among the employees. This, of course, increased the material interest of the employees in the performance of the enterprise.

The scheme of revenue distribution changed again in the first part of 1961.[62] This new scheme may be represented in the following way:

From *total revenue* are subtracted the costs of materials and amortization.

From the remaining *income* are subtracted interest of 6 per cent on capital, rent and other contributions, and turnover tax.

The remainder is *gross profit.* From this is subtracted the 15 per cent Federal tax.

This leaves the *net profit.* This has four divisions: (1) payroll, (2) the working capital fund, (3) the collective consumption fund, and (4) the reserve fund. The combined amount of the working capital fund and the collective consumption fund is subject to a 20 per cent tax which goes into the investment funds of the local government and the republic in which the enterprise is located; they split the amount equally. The payroll includes, besides the amount actually paid out to the workers, three other items: a 4 per cent assessment for communal buildings, a 22 per cent payment for social security, and a 15 per cent tax which is split equally between the budget of the local government and the budget of the republic.

The most original feature of the scheme of 1961 was a new treatment of the wage bill — it became a part of the firm's profits. Hence, the crucial problem upon which the operational value of the whole concept depended was the distribution of net profits between the wage fund and the internal funds of the firm. An attempt was made to leave this problem entirely up to the Workers' Councils. The resulting tendency of wages to increase sharply and the development of a very grave problem with respect to the short-term liquidity of the firms convinced the government that short-run material gains mean more to the workers of Yugoslavia than long-run prospects, and on April 18, 1962, the Law on Distribution of Net Profits of Enterprises[63] was instituted. This law solved the problem of distribution of net profits between the wage fund and the internal funds by introducing a complicated guideline:

$$W = \frac{\text{net profit}}{1 + XY},$$

where Y is the productivity coefficient and X equals the ratio of internal funds to the wage bill (I/W) and is calculated for any given year ($X_1$) from data for the previous year ($X_0$) in the following way: $X_1 = (K_1/K_0)X_0$, where K equals capital per worker.

The immense analytical importance of this guideline will be further considered in Chapter IV.

*Formation and Liquidation of the Enterprise.* The Law on Government Commercial Enterprises of August 2, 1946,[64] classified all enterprises as being of federal, republic, and local significance. By this law all enterprises were put under the control of the federal, republic, or local government, and, furthermore, only these three governments could form new enterprises. This division of enterprises was abandoned in 1957 when all enterprises were transferred to the domain of their local governments. The Law on Government Commercial Enterprises stated that the government in control of an enterprise should appoint the administrative superior of the enterprise, who in turn appoints the director of the enterprise.

The Law on Formation and Operations of Enterprises of January 30, 1952,[65] stated that a new enterprise can only be formed by the government on the initiative of the government, cooperatives, commercial associations, or groups of consumers. It further provided that an enterprise can expand and open branches in every locality, subject to the approval of the local government.

A new law on the formation and liquidation of enterprises was announced on December 24, 1953.[66] It stated that a new enterprise can be formed by the government, commercial associations, social organizations, cooperatives, and groups of citizens. It is no longer the government that forms a new enterprise on its own or someone else's initiative. Well-defined legal entities such as commercial associations, cooperatives, and groups of citizens were given the right to form a new enterprise subject to government approval. Furthermore, the law said, the government could not deny its approval if the legal requirements were met. These requirements were that the new enterprise would engage in no activities except those which the permit was asked for, that the enterprise was equipped with the minimum of sanitary facilities, that the enterprise would be able to hire the necessary minimum of highly skilled employees, and that the founders provided the enterprise with an adequate amount of fixed and circulating capital to start operating. However, the law said, when a group of citizens asks for a permit to form an enterprise, the government has the right to deny it even if all legal requirements have been met.

This law also changed the procedure for appointing the director. The director was to be appointed on a competitive basis by the commission on appointments. Two-thirds of the commission members were to be selected by the local government and one-third by the Workers' Council of the enterprise. The contest had to be announced in the *Official Bulletin* and had to specify the qualifications and experience needed for the job. (See Appendix VI for typical announcements.)

On July 22, 1962, it was announced that a firm already established in one locality may open branches anywhere in Yugoslavia, without seeking the permission of the local government. This action meant the end of local monopolies, which more often than not were protected by the local governments.[67]

Termination of enterprises was regulated by the government by the law of December 26, 1951.[68] A more elaborate law on the termination of enterprises was announced on December 24, 1953.[69] This law distinguished between regular and compulsory liquidation. Regular liquidation is ordered by the government when the economic reasons for the existence of the enterprise have disappeared (e.g., the government will order regular liquidation of a mine when its reserves have been exhausted) or when the enterprise gets involved in an activity other than its legal one (e.g., the government will close down an enterprise producing bicycles if it starts producing radios). Compulsory liquidation is ordered by the court when the enterprise cannot meet payments on the right of use or when the enterprise cannot meet a financial obligation whose settlement was ordered by the court.

The announcement of the liquidation of an enterprise has to be made public in the *Official Bulletin* (see Appendix VI) and it has to invite all those who have unsettled claims on the enterprise to report them to the local government (in the case of regular liquidation) or to the court (in the case of compulsory liquidation). The law also said that capital in possession of the enterprise cannot be used for satisfaction of the claims. The local government is supposed to take that over before the procedure of liquidation begins. This is legally justified; no claim can be satisfied from assets over which the enterprise has no ownership rights. And since Yugoslavia is a socialist country, in which by definition capital is publicly owned, the logic of this provision is clear.

In the case of compulsory liquidation the law provided the order in which unsettled claims should be satisfied: (1) unpaid social contributions, (2) social security obligations, (3) claims of the banks, (4) other claims, (5) claims of the employees for their earnings. The apparent discrimination against the employees must be interpreted in the context of the whole organizational framework of the Yugoslav economy. Since mid-1950 the pattern of legal changes has been to identify the interest of the workers with that of the enterprise. The workers were invited to participate in the gains of their enterprises and were, consequently, expected to take the risk of potential losses. This provision is, in fact, a strong incentive for the workers to fight for the realization of their legal rights to manage the enterprise, because only then can they, by their own actions, safeguard their material conditions.

*Labor Relations in the Yugoslav Enterprise.* The first Law on Labor Relations was enacted on October 2, 1948.[70] It contained a number of provisions related to the hiring and firing of employees. The law stated that employment can be terminated for the following reasons: unjustifiable absence from work for more than three days; unjustifiable tardiness; undisclosed mental or physical handicap at the time of hiring; and court order. Hiring is done, according to this law, by the director of the enterprise.

A very comprehensive Law on Labor Relations was enacted on December 25, 1957,[71] and amended several times during 1958 and 1959. This law contained 420 articles. Some of its basic features are:

1. Hiring is done by the Workers' Council, which is the highest managing organ of an enterprise.

2. The employee has to be over 15 years of age and mentally and physically able to do the particular work for which he is being hired.

3. The director cannot do the hiring but can make suggestions as to the hiring.

4. Vacation is granted to a worker after eleven months of work. The worker does not have to remain employed by the same firm to be eligible for vacation. He can change jobs as often as he pleases, and provided that the intervals between two jobs were no longer than fifteen days, he may have his vacation eleven months after starting the first job. The minimum vacation is two weeks for those with less than five years of work, while

the maximum is five weeks for those with more than twenty-five years of employment.

5. For a breach of discipline an employee can be punished in one of the following ways: reminder, strong reminder, public reminder, cut in salary up to 10 per cent for a maximum of three months, transfer to another job within the enterprise, and firing. The director should investigate and punish an employee for a breach of discipline, but the employee may appeal to the Workers' Council.

6. Employment cannot be terminated by a one-sided decision of the enterprise in case of pregnancy, sickness, army service, or participation in public works.

7. In case of a decline in production the enterprise may lay off the necessary number of workers. However, the procedure is long and complicated. The director may lay off an employee but the employee may appeal the director's decision to the Workers' Council. If the Council confirms the director's decision the employee can send his complaint to a commission formed by the local government. The commission's decision is final. The laid-off worker receives unemployment insurance from the local government until it finds him work in his trade. Obviously, the commission has every reason to consider complaints by laid-off workers carefully.

*Legal Acts Concerning Productivity of Labor.* The Law on Inventions and Technical Improvements was enacted on December 15, 1948.[72] The purpose of the law was to encourage new inventions, defined as new combinations of the agents of production. The state, according to this law, had to provide adequate grants and laboratories and also to give prizes to inventors. On June 7, 1961,[73] the Law on the Yugoslav Institute for Labor Productivity was enacted. The law said that this institute, a self-financing entity whose revenue is payments for suggestions and advice extended to its clients, was to engage primarily in the analysis of the impact of organizational and technical changes in the social, political, and economic spheres on the rate of economic development and productivity improvement.

The pattern of legal changes in Yugoslavia indicates the emergence of market instruments, notably that of profitability of investment, in allocating the country's resources.

We can distinguish three major structural innovations in the Yugoslav economy, each of which was followed by a cluster of smaller structural changes. The first innovation, in 1946, introduced deterministic and administrative relationships between the productive units themselves, between the productive units and the financial institutions, and between the productive units and the government. The second innovation, that of 1950–51, drastically reduced the scope of administrative relations between the productive units themselves and between the productive units and the banking system. The third innovation, in 1961 – still in the process of being worked out – attempts to increase the importance of market prices and to reduce the scope of administrative relationships between the productive units and the government in the sphere of income distribution.

Finally, the analysis of the legal structure of the Yugoslav economy shows that its performance since 1954 has been increasingly dependent upon the ability of the banking system to make the Social Plan workable, and in particular to meet the challenge of developing a rational and efficient evaluation of investment projects.

# II ECONOMIC PLANNING IN YUGOSLAVIA

ECONOMIC planning can be defined as a deliberate choice of economic priorities. The institution of economic planning is probably as old as the institution of government, if not older. Today, there seems to exist a general agreement about the necessity of some planning in the allocation of resources.

While the scope and method of economic planning differ from one country to another, there seem to be three major types of economic planning today: in Western Europe and the United States planning is characterized by various degrees of government interference with economic processes; in Yugoslavia, India, Egypt, and some African and Asian countries planning tends to be limited to the macroeconomic variables; and in the U.S.S.R. and most Eastern European countries economic planners strive to control the allocation of resources on both the macroeconomic and the microeconomic level.

The most recent discussion going on in the U.S.S.R. and Czechoslovakia indicates that there exists a strong possibility that those countries may adopt, at some future date, the second type of planning mentioned above. In the text I shall refer to the second and third types of planning as the investment plan and the production plan respectively.*

In capitalist countries economic planning is done through government interference – mostly indirect – with the processes of production and distribution. These interferences may be temporary, such as an occasional imposition of price controls, or permanent, such as the institution of taxation and its changing structure. The tools used by the government to

*Though the Soviet system of planning may be changed, as noted above, my references to Soviet conditions should be understood as pertaining to the period up to 1965.

interfere with the processes of production and distribution have either aggregate or reallocative effects or both. To mention a few:

1. Changes in the quantity of money are expected to have impact on the *aggregates*, such as total investment outlays, total consumption, and total income. If this is so, the government can hope to stimulate a chosen rate of economic growth through changing the supply of money.[1]

2. A corporate tax has a reallocative effect because it makes product prices in the corporate sector of the economy higher, and prices in the noncorporate sector of the economy lower, than their equilibrium levels would have been if the tax were nondiscriminatory.[2]

3. Commodity taxes have an obvious *reallocative effect.*

4. Progressive income taxes are believed to stimulate higher consumption. But even if this were not the case, the progressive income tax would still have some *reallocative* effect on the composition of output.

5. Government expenditures for goods and services can have both aggregate and reallocative effects on the national output.

6. In some countries (France, for example) governments make comprehensive surveys of the intentions of investors and of consumers, and of the availability of resources, in order to decrease excessive and wasteful use of resources by improving the flow of information.

Thus, government planning in capitalist countries aims to remedy the "undesired effects" of competition in imperfect markets by influencing the size and distribution of national income.

Economic planning in the U.S.S.R.[3] determines minimum production quotas for the economy as a whole, for each industry, and for each enterprise. To make these production quotas attainable the government needs full and tight control over the use of the country's productive resources. Hence, the production plan presupposes and, in fact, embodies a detailed plan of the allocation of resources. This scheme naturally does not leave much room for market decisions, since prices based on the interaction of demand and supply would be wholly irrational as far as the fulfillment of the plan was concerned.

This system of production planning has been exposed to sharp criticism, the most damaging being from the Austrian school. Professor Novakovich of Belgrade University summarized the "Austrian criticism" under three closely interrelated headings:[4] (1) the central planning board lacks meaningful objective criteria for its decisions concerning the structure of production, consumption, and the rate and pattern of investment; (2)

the price system in a centrally planned economy fails to convey the urgency of human wants; and (3) consequently, the ultimate purpose of the production and its rationality are, at the least, extremely vague. Without denying the logic of the Austrian criticism, Professor Novakovich points out what he believes to be their major methodological mistake: the Austrian criticism was unjustly turned against socialism in general, though it was in fact directed only against the system of centralized production planning, which is one but certainly not the definitive or exclusive form of the socialist economy.

Professor Novakovich emphasizes that East European economists still maintain that a detailed production plan is *the* best method of planning, while the Yugoslav economists have come to the conclusion that within the broad framework of the economic plan the market mechanism should be allowed to bring about the optimal allocation of resources. The result of this point of view has been the emergence of investment planning in Yugoslavia.

## THE YUGOSLAV SYSTEM OF PLANNING BEFORE AND AFTER 1953–54

In this section the analysis will concentrate on the form and content of the First Five Year Plan,[5] which stemmed from the Law on Economic Plan and Government Planning Agencies of 1946, and the Social Plan for 1962, which is based on the principles of the Law on Planned Management of the National Economy of 1952.*

To make the qualitative differences between the two methods of planning clear the best approach seems to be to fall back on the original language of each of the two plans. Therefore, some selected passages will be quoted as they appeared in the original texts (my italics).

### Selections from *The Law on the Five Year Plan for the Development of the National Economy of the Federative People's Republic of Yugoslavia in the Period from 1947 to 1951*

#### PART ONE: THE TASKS OF THE FIVE YEAR PLAN

CHAPTER I: The Basic Tasks of the Five Year Plan

Article 1, 2) To mobilize and constantly strengthen all sources of

*In his book Albert Waterston has covered all technical details concerning the process of implementation of the plan. Since his book is a complete descriptive document on economic planning in Yugoslavia, I shall refrain from unnecessary repetition of the descriptive features of Yugoslav planning. See Waterston, *Planning in Yugoslavia* (Baltimore: Johns Hopkins University Press, 1962).

accumulation. To invest 278.3 milliard dinars in the national economy during the period 1947–1951.

3) *To increase* the value of the total production from 116.5 milliards in 1939 to 266.7 milliards in 1951, which means increasing the value of pre-war production more than 2¼ times.

8) *To increase* the production of means of production . . . from 43% of the total industrial output in 1939 to 57% in 1951.

13) To link up working craftsmen with planned construction and production. *To ensure* raw materials, tools and work to working craftsmen. *To organize* a fair system of distribution of raw materials and supervise their consumption.

14) *To ensure* material and organisational assistance to artisan cooperatives.

Article 2, 11) *To ensure* material and technical assistance to existing and newly-founded peasant working cooperatives. . . . To introduce production schemes and financial plans. . . . To improve the organization of their work.

Article 3, 2) *To introduce* a fair system of technical and economic norms of production. . . .

4) To elaborate and introduce a differential system of wages, salaries and bonuses for the fulfilment and surpassing of the plan. . . .

Article 5, 1) To ensure a speedier tempo of development in the economically backward republics and remove all consequences of uneven development. . . .

Article 8: Investments. Value of new investment for the period 1947–1951 (in milliard dinars):

| | |
|---|---|
| Total | 278.3 |
| Mining and metallurgy | 30.8 |
| Production of electric power | 30.0 |
| Industry | 54.9 |
| Building enterprises | 3.5 |
| Agriculture | 19.4 |
| Forestry | 3.6 |
| Communications | 72.6 |
| Trade | 7.8 |
| Unproductive branches | 55.7 |

CHAPTER II: Plan For the Development of Productive Forces

Article 10, 22) *To increase* the output of iron ore to 1.5 million tons in 1951. To this end to develop and mechanize the mines of Ljubija and Varesh.

26) *To increase* the output of lead to 65,000 tons by enlarging the foundry at Trepcha in the second half of 1948.

33) To construct a factory of light machines in Zagreb, a factory of medium machines in Sarajevo and a factory of heavy machines in Belgrade.

41) To start the manufacture of lead cables in the Belgrade district and by 1951 reach an output of 10,000 tons.

CHAPTER III: The Plan for Raising the Material and Cultural Level of the People

Article 14, 1) To ensure a steady increase in the productivity of work.

2) *To increase the number of skilled workers* from 350,000 in 1946 to 750,000 in 1951.

3) *To ensure the increase* of the cadres with secondary professional training from 65,000 in 1946 to 150,000 in 1951.

4) *To ensure an increase* in the number of experts with university qualifications to an average of 5,000 annually.

CHAPTER IV: The Removal of Unevenness in the Economic Development of the People's Republics

CHAPTER V: The Plan for the Economic Development of the People's Republics

Article 24, People's Republic of Slovenia: *To increase* the output of cast iron to 9,520 tons in 1951. *To produce* 50,000 bicycles in 1951 and introduce the manufacture of typewriters, *producing 10,000. To produce 6,300* cubic metres of plywood in 1951. . . . To achieve a production of 3,000 tons of first quality tinned fruits and vegetables in 1951.

PART TWO: COORDINATED PLANS

CHAPTER VI: Plan of Production According to Branches

Article 34: Plan of Commerce and Supply

| *Industrial Supplies* | *1951* | *Percentage of Increase (1946 = 100)* |
|---|---|---|
| Cotton fabrics (mil. metres) | 186 | 189 |
| Woollen fabrics (mil. metres) | 20 | 105 |
| Leather footwear (1000 pairs) | 7,780 | 136 |
| Rubber footwear (1000 pairs) | 3,200 | 91 |
| Rubber peasant shoes (1000 pairs) | 4,400 | 550 |
| Tobacco (tons) | 16,000 | 128 |
| Salt (100 metric quintals) | 17,687 | 133 |
| Soap (100 metric quintals) | 2,800 | 157 |
| Paper (100 metric quintals) | 4,255 | 127 |
| Matches (million boxes) | 304 | 127 |
| Electric bulbs (1000) | 3,200 | 640 |

CHAPTER VII: Basic Plan of Production in the People's Republics

| *Beer (1000 hectalitres)* | *1939* | *1951* | *Percentage of Increase (1939 = 1946 = 100)* |
|---|---|---|---|
| Total | 426.6 | 1,040 | 243 |
| Serbia | 272.5 | 523 | 192 |

| | | | |
|---|---|---|---|
| Croatia | 68.9 | 205 | 298 |
| Slovenia | 65 | 127 | 195 |
| Bosnia and Herzegovina | | 109 | |
| Macedonia | | 60 | |
| Montenegro | | 16 | |

CHAPTER VIII: Raising of the Standard of Living

*Number of meals* served people in restaurants: 140,000,000 in 1951
Plan for lowering cost-prices:

| | *Reduction of Cost Prices (per cent)* | *Increased Productivity (per cent)* |
|---|---|---|
| Textile industry | 30 | 55 |
| Leather and footwear industry | 15.3 | 67 |
| Rubber industry | 25 | 57 |
| Food industry | 20 | 60 |
| Radio industry | 40 | ... |

The *costs of trade* in 1951 *will be* 10% less than the retail selling prices.

PART THREE: THE CARRYING OUT AND FULFILMENT OF THE PLAN

CHAPTER IX

Article 40: The Government of the Federative People's Republic of Yugoslavia will undertake *all measures necessary* for the realization of this plan.

The government will . . . ensure the participation of the broad masses of the people in the carrying out of the five year plan . . .

Article 41: The carrying out of the tasks and duties . . . is *the duty* and privilege *of every citizen* of the Federative People's Republic of Yugoslavia.

Article 42: In performing their tasks . . . all economic units in the State, cooperative and private sectors of the national economy will enjoy equal rights as regards obtaining the means and conditions necessary for the carrying out of their tasks.

By economic and other measures the State will assist cooperative organizations and private producers, especially peasants and craftsmen, to carry out the tasks set in the economic plans.

[Article 45] *All* economic and other planned *activities* . . . of organs of the State institutions and enterprises, and other institutions, organizations and citizens thereto enjoined by this law and other existing laws and regulations, *must be coordinated with the tasks laid down in this law.*

An examination of these selections reveals the following main characteristics of the First Five Year Plan.

1. The plan set a *lump sum of investment* and provided for its breakdown into nine economic branches.

2. The plan determined the *pattern of investment.*

3. The plan set rigid *production plans.* The production plans included *the exact quantities to be produced by different economic branches* (for example, 4,400,000 pairs of rubber peasant shoes were to be produced in 1951, and that quota was determined back in 1947); *the quantity of production by the various People's Republics* (the plan said that in Slovenia 10,000 typewriters should be produced in 1951); *the number of workers and employees* in various skills to be "produced" by 1951; *the building of new plants at predetermined locations*; and *production quotas for each enterprise.*

4. Distribution of supply to individual enterprises, cooperatives, and artisans was rigidly planned.

5. The plan determined the exact rate of productivity increase by industrial branches.

6. Prices were fixed by the government.

The language used by the legislature in setting different goals is worth noting; it is the language of orders and commands.

The Five Year Plan was not nearly fulfilled in 1951, and it was extended for another year.

The Yugoslavs changed their system of planning in 1952, and introduced the so-called "Social Plan." Since 1952 a Social Plan has been enacted each year in addition to long-range plans for the periods from 1957–61 and 1961–65. On the following pages selected passages illustrating basic properties of the plan for 1962 are quoted; we shall see how it differs from the First Five Year Plan.

## Selections from *The Social Plan for 1962* [6]

### PART ONE: BASIC PROPOSITIONS OF THE SOCIAL PLAN FOR 1962

CHAPTER I: Assessment of Economic Movements in the Year 1961

The development of economy during the year 1961 . . . had assumed a slower tempo . . . The 1961 Plan had also reckoned with a certain slowing-down of production, but the tempo of production had been slowed-down more than had been expected. The rate of growth of social product, it is estimated, will amount to about 5.5 per cent.

Industrial production, whose increase had been planned to be 12%, will not increase by more than 9%.

The achieved volume of agricultural production is smaller by about 20% than the volume set in the 1961 Plan.

The main causes of such a movement of . . . production were: (a) certain lack of structural coordination between production and consumption, and the slow progress in agricultural production and its limited absorption abilities, which had rendered difficult the sale of products in certain branches and production groups (metal processing industry, electric industry, etc.); (b) insufficient supply of the circulating capital for economic enterprises . . . (c) most of the year passed in adapting our industry to the important changes which have been carried out in the system of distribution of incomes.

The average real pay in the entire socialist sector of economy had increased by about 5%, while productivity of labor was increased by 3.9%.

The general index of wholesale prices shifted up by 9.15 . . . the cost of living increased by 9%.

The increase in prices had been considerably due to certain deliberate interventions, such as the change in foreign currency rates, price corrections, etc. But the differences between available cash and available commodities, which occurred in both the personal consumption and in the production market, also had an influence on the increase in prices and market instability.

CHAPTER II: The Basic Propositions of the Economic Policy for the Year 1962

The most important aim of the economic policy is to accelerate the tempo of production.

A faster growth of industrial production should therefore, be achieved by removing the obstacles which in the year 1961 had held back production . . . by bigger and more adequate supply of circulating capital, by easing the sale conditions, by a more flexible adaptation of the structure of production to the requirements of consumption and of the market.

Increase in agricultural production . . . will assume a special importance in 1962.

Restoration of balance between cash and commodities and stability of market and prices are most closely connected with realization of the tasks which have been set in the field of production.

Real personal income in economy should grow in harmony with the growth of productivity of labor.

Enterprise shall make increase in personal incomes in line with the results of economic activities achieved on the basis of higher productivity of labor . . . the increase in revenue which comes about because of the price movements or changes in regulations should not, as a rule, be used for increases in personal incomes.

To ensure in all branches and activities a quicker completion of the projects on hand.

To provide . . . larger funds . . . for . . . those investments which expand production of basic raw materials and of reproduction of materials and which increase production for exports.

To increase investments in the underdeveloped regions of the country.

The most important task that presents itself in the year 1962 in the field of foreign trade is that of maximum increase in export of industrial articles.

With respect to imports, it shall be necessary to strive towards a most economical use of foreign exchange.

## PART TWO: GUIDELINES FOR DEVELOPMENT OF ECONOMY IN 1962

### CHAPTER III: Social Gross Product, Social Product and National Income

Proceeding [from] the size of available production capacities, availability of labor force and possibility of growth of productivity of labor, and counting with the planned amount of exports, *it is estimated* that in the year 1962 the following real growth of social gross product, social product and national income will be achieved: (in billions of dinars at the constant 1959 prices)

| | *1960* | *1961* | *1962* | *1961 ÷ 1960* | *1962 ÷ 1961* | *1962 ÷ 1960* |
|---|---|---|---|---|---|---|
| Social gross product | 5,849 | 6,278 | 7,116 | 107.3 | 113.3 | 121.7 |
| Social product | 2,757 | 2,909 | 3,370 | 105.5 | 115.8 | 122.2 |
| National income | 2,559 | 2,683 | 3,118 | 104.9 | 116.2 | 121.8 |

*It is estimated* that in 1962 the movement . . . of various economic branches . . . of employment and of productivity of labor in the socialist sector will be as follows (1961 = 100):

| | *Social Product* | *Employment* | *Productivity* |
|---|---|---|---|
| Total economy | 113.3 | 106.2 | 106.7 |
| Industry | 113 | 105.4 | 107.2 |
| Agriculture | 135.6 | 107.6 | 126 |
| Forestry | 114.2 | 111.4 | 102.5 |
| Building trade | 112.4 | 103.6 | 108.5 |
| Transport | 111.3 | 103.6 | 107.4 |
| Commerce and hotel industry | 111.1 | 107.2 | 103.6 |
| Handicrafts | 114.2 | 109.9 | 103.9 |

The following economic-political aims should be achieved by the basic distribution of social product and available funds in the year 1962:

1. Reduction of deficit in the balance of payments.

2. The increase in . . . personal consumption . . . should . . . grow.

3. Commercial investments should . . . increase at a slower rate than the rate at which available funds are growing.

### CHAPTER IV: Investment

Of the total funds projected for investments, about 1,163,000,000,000 dinars will be invested in fixed assets funds of which 847,000,000,000 in commercial, 316,000,000,000 in non-commercial purposes, and about 270,000,000,000 dinars in circulating capital funds. The investments in circulating capital are set at a level higher than the investments made in the year 1961 for about 14%.

[Investments expenditures of the enterprises are expected to amount up to 33.3 per cent of the total investment in fixed assets.]

The following structure of investments, by economic branches, *is envisaged*:

| | | *Per Cent of Total* | *Rate of Growth (1961 = 100)* |
|---|---|---|---|
| Industry and mining | 443,000,000,000 | 51.7 | 113.3 |
| Agriculture | 123,000,000,000 | 14.7 | 115.0 |
| Forestry | 15,000,000,000 | 1.8 | 107.1 |
| Building trade | 25,000,000,000 | 3.0 | 104.2 |
| Transport | 175,000,000,000 | 20.9 | 102.3 |
| Commerce and hotel industry | 50,000,000,000 | 6.0 | 104.2 |
| Handicrafts | 16,000,000,000 | 1.9 | 106.7 |

CHAPTER V: Personal Consumption and Living Standard

*It is anticipated* that the amount of personal consumption of the total population in the year 1962 will be higher by 7.9 per cent and that per capita consumption will be up by 6.7 per cent.

CHAPTER VI: Budgets.

The Federal Budget expenditures will increase from 580,603,000,000 in 1961 to 634,695,000,000 in 1962, or by 9.3 per cent.

Most of the increase in the Federal Budget expenditures is for repayment of foreign loans and for grants to the People's Republic of Bosnia and Herzegovina, the People's Republic of Macedonia and the People's Republic of Montenegro, as well as the Autonomous Region of Kosovo and Metohija.

CHAPTER VII: Economic Relations with Foreign Countries

In the year 1962, it shall be necessary, in the case of new investments from all sources, to pay attention more than in previous years to increase in production of articles intended for export and to greater profitability of this production.

CHAPTER VIII: Market and Prices

For market stabilization, it is of particular importance that the planned volume and structure of production and exports be achieved, that the planned level of all forms of consumption be maintained, and that personal incomes in economy be harmonized as much as possible with the growth of productivity of labor.

## PART THREE: DEVELOPMENT OF ECONOMIC PARTICULAR SECTORS

### CHAPTER IX: Manufacturing

Industrial production should achieve in the year 1962 a rate of growth of 13%, and it is of a decisive importance that this growth be achieved with a relatively smaller increase in import of raw materials and a considerable acceleration of exports of industrial products.

Such a task . . . demands . . . the making of efforts in the direction of increasing of production in those branches and production groups which are based on domestic raw materials sources and which, with relatively small imports, participate to a considerable extent in exports or replace essential imports . . . Therefore the greatest possible volume of production should be achieved in oil industry, in ferrous and non-ferrous metallurgy in lumber industry and generally in wood processing industry, in basic chemical industry and in industry for processing of agricultural products.

Proceeding from . . . basic orientations in production, the following movement is anticipated by various . . . industrial branches and important groups of products.

| *Textile Industry* | *Realized* *1960* | *Production* *1961* | *Plan* *1962* |
|---|---|---|---|
| Indices of growth | 114 | 106 | 118 |
| Cotton yarn (thou. tons) | 52.7 | 58.9 | 75.6 |
| Cotton and artificial fabrics (mill. sq. metres) | 269.2 | 281.1 | 336.0 |
| Woolen fabrics (mill. sq. metres) | 32.7 | 30.3 | 33.0 |
| Silk fabrics (mill. sq. metres) | 20.0 | 23.1 | 26.7 |

### CHAPTER X: Agriculture

Agricultural production in the year 1962 should be increased by 23% compared with the low production in 1961 . . . The more favorable material conditions than had existed in the two preceding years, will constitute basis for increase in crop farming production in 1962. . . . It is estimated that during the year 1962 they will have at their disposal about 6,000 new tractors and 1,400 combine harvesters . . . The amount of guaranteed deposit . . . from the General Investment Fund will be reduced, both in case of loans for expansion . . . of new areas of land, and in case of investments which ensure higher production of high quality products which are greatly in demand.

## PART FOUR: MEASURES FOR EXECUTION OF THE PLAN AND THE FUNDS REGIME

### CHAPTER XII: Measures for Execution of the Plan

The responsible authorities should study and undertake measures for elimination of appearances of excessive contracting of debts without coverage and financing between economic organizations and other organs, as well as between economic organizations themselves.

That all agencies from whose funds investments are made in fixed assets also make adequate investments in circulating capital.

That the responsible authorities study and undertake measures in the direction of normalization of the tempo of production of coal and its delivery to wholesalers.

That the responsible authorities introduce a long-term regime of financing of oil prospecting and opening of oil fields.

That the granting of investment credits from social funds be made on the basis of a thorough examination of the applications for credits of agricultural organizations; the credits should assure increase in production.

CHAPTER XIII: Investments and Funds

The General Investment Fund: The money for the General Investment Fund shall come from:

1) The contributions from the income of economic enterprises which belongs to the Federation—up to 40.3%. [The rest goes into the federal budget.]

2) The income from the tax on extra profits—up to 40.3%.

3) The income from the interest on loans and credits granted for circulating capital to the amount of 9,300,000,000 dinars.

4) The income from foreign exchange calculated at the settlement rate, made in 1962 and deriving from loans and other foreign arrangements intended for the financing of investments.

5) Other incomes.

The money from the General Investment Fund will be used:

For investments in fixed assets: 384,000,000,000 dinars, as follows:

| | |
|---|---|
| Industry and mining | 200,000,000,000 |
| War industry | 3,000,000,000* |
| Agriculture | 75,000,000,000 |
| Forestry | 2,000,000,000 |
| Building trade | 4,000,000,000 |
| Transport and communications | 66,000,000,000 |
| Commerce, hotels, tourism | 3,500,000,000 |
| Other investments | 21,500,000,000 |
| For production for export | 10,000,000,000 |

*National defense is financed primarily through the budget.

For investments in circulating capital: 60,000,000,000

The money from the General Investment Fund earmarked for investments in industry and mining shall be used by the Yugoslav Investment Bank and the Yugoslav Agricultural Bank:

1) For the meeting their obligations under the already concluded loans in previous years.

2) For the granting of the new loans to the following branches: ferrous

metallurgy, coal which will ensure the planned development of ferrous metallurgy, oil—especially for the opening of oil and natural gas fields, for the development of cement works, chemical industry, non-ferrous metallurgy, and electro-economy especially to the laying of HT lines and building 220 KV transformer stations.

3) For the meeting of their obligations in connection with the guaranteed investments on the territories of the People's Republics of Macedonia, Montenegro and the Autonomous Region of Kosovo and Motohija.

4) For reconstruction and adaptation of production plans for the purpose of improvement of production for export.

The money in the General Investment Fund earmarked for loans for circulating capital of economic enterprises shall be given as loans, by the Yugoslav Investment Bank and the Yugoslav Agricultural Bank, to those applicants whose fixed assets are financed, totally or partially from the General Investment Fund.

CHAPTER XIV: The Credit Policy Measures

The total growth of circulating capital in economy in 1962 should reach a level corresponding to the growth of the social gross product envisaged by this plan.

The National Bank shall provide funds for the increase in the amount of consumer credits in 1962.

The banks should give special priority in . . . granting . . . the credits in 1962 to those enterprises which increase production for export.

CHAPTER XVII: Market Regulations Measures

The Federal Executive Council . . . may

1) fix prices and method of price formation for goods and services.

3) introduce regulations on coordination of transport rates.

5) in the case of imports of goods and services prescribe exemption from obligations towards the society.

CHAPTER XVIII: Concluding Provisions

The plans of enterprises *should be in harmony* with the aims and tasks of this Social Plan.

Some of the notable features of this document are:

1. The Social Plan for 1962 uses "exact" language only when it quotes the amounts of the G.I.F. allocated by branches. When it comes to the sum total of all investments (because of the uncertainty concerning the amount of internal financing by enterprises) and to its structural distribution (because the plan cannot be certain where demand will be strong and who will have more funds for internal financing), the plan uses the language of "anticipations."

2. The Social Plan leaves the distribution of money from the G.I.F. to the banks and directs them to allocate the money in accordance with a number of criteria (see Ch. I). The plan clearly underwrites the power of the banking system.

3. The Yugoslav enterprise has to buy its supplies in the market. The plan does not provide them.

4. The Social Plan does not impose production quotas on individual enterprises. Each enterprise is free to determine the quantity and quality of its output.

5. The incentive for producing goods demanded by the market is found in the provision that firms may distribute a part of their earnings among the employees.

### THE PRODUCTION PLAN AND THE INVESTMENT PLAN

To clarify the significant qualitative differences between the two types of planning, the production plan and the investment plan, we must consider two major questions: (1) How does the economic plan determine the basic division of national product between consumption and investment? (By consumption we shall mean production of consumer goods and short-term credits for enlarging this production.) (2) How does the government secure the most efficient use of scarce resources?

Let us assume full employment of both capital and labor, constant technology, the production function $Z = K^{1/2}, L^{1/2}$, and given relative factor prices. From these assumptions a diagram similar to the so-called Edgeworth's Box[7] can be drawn (see Fig. 2) showing different production possibilities in consumption goods industries (X) and in investment goods industries (Y). $O_xO_y$ is the production scale line representing the most efficient combination of the factors of production employed in producing X and Y. On any isoquant curve (X or Y) the quantity of X (or Y) produced is constant. Therefore $\Delta X$ (or $\Delta Y$) $= 0$. If the marginal physical product of capital in producing X is $MPP_{kx}$, the marginal physical product of labor in producing X is $MPP_{lx}$ and the corresponding factors for producing Y are $MPP_{ky}$ and $MPP_{ly}$, then, given relative factor prices, the condition of technological efficiency is satisfied when

$$\frac{P_k \times MPP_{kx}}{P_l \times MPP_{lx}} = \frac{P_k \times MPP_{ky}}{P_l \times MPP_{ly}}.$$

This condition is satisfied at any point on the $O_xO_y$ scale to mean that the economy could supply more of X only by producing less of Y or

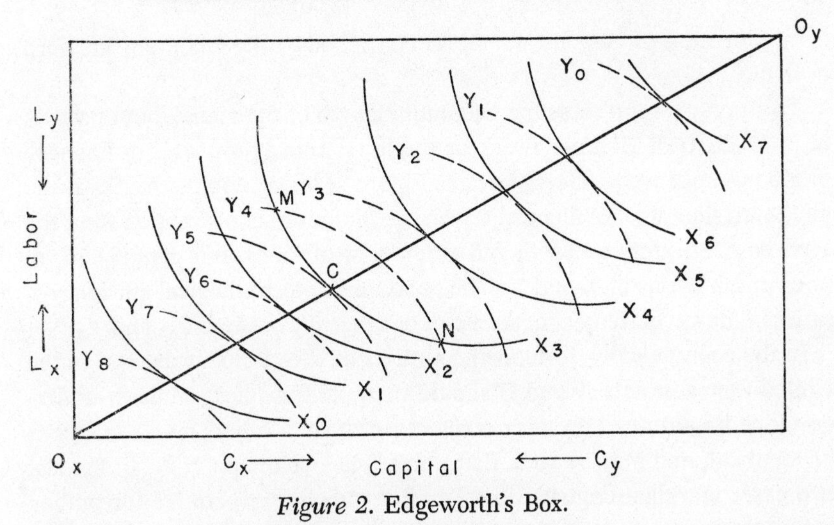


*Figure* 2. Edgeworth's Box.

vice versa. We can now convert the production scale line into the production possibility curve in Figure 3.

In the circular flow of economic life the economy would tend to reinvest only that amount of its national product which would be equal to wear and tear on the existing capital goods. We denote this as point A (arbitrarily chosen) on the lower part of the $O_xO_y$ curve in Figure 3. This is the minimum level of investment in the long run. The maximum level



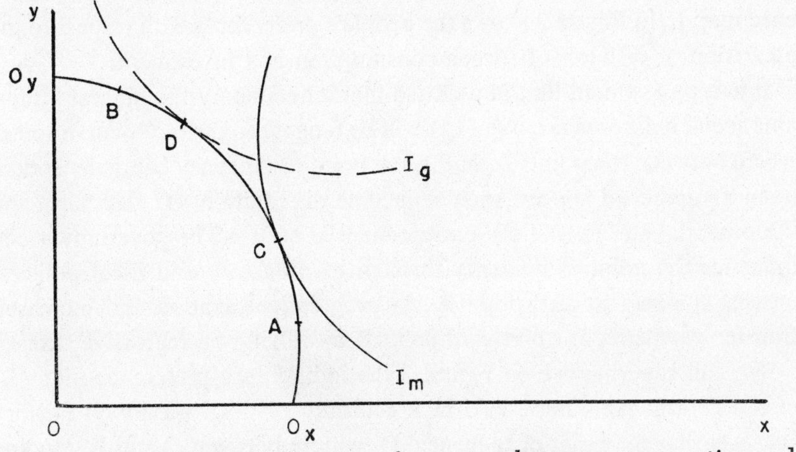


*Figure* 3. The problem of allocation of resources between consumption and investment, $I_m$ representing the highest attainable social indifference curve and $I_g$ the highest governmental indifference curve.

of investment is set at point B, and is determined by the minimum standard of living.

This point B represents the maximum length of the roundabout process of production of Böhm-Bawerk or the maximum "time we can finance" production of Jevons. Going back to Figure 2, let us assume that $X_3$ is the minimum time we can finance. Given the minimum consumption fund the economy can produce (with full employent of labor and capital) m, n, or c combinations of X and Y. The condition of technological efficiency is satisfied, however, only at c, the point of tangency between $X_3$ and $Y_5$.

In the economically developed countries of Western Europe and in the United States, points A and B should be quite far apart, while in underdeveloped countries they may come close to each other, may sometimes be identical, and may be such that point B lies below point A. In the last two cases marginal contributions from outside are imperative for pulling the country out of stagnation,[8] because "an economy can devote to real investment . . . the surplus of consumer goods production over what is consumed by the producers of these goods themselves."[9] A developed economy will, of course, find this surplus large, while an underdeveloped economy may experience trouble in getting its net investment greater than zero.

To analyze the problem of allocation of scarce resources, let us assume the size and distribution of national income, the price level and relative prices, and the tax structure as given. Then the social indifference-preference map $I_m$ in Figure 3 shows the people's preferences with respect to the allocation of resources between consumption and investment.

It can be assumed that in a closed market economy the highest attainable social indifference curve ($I_m$) will be tangent to the $O_xO_y$ curve somewhere between the points A and B, the point of tangency being dependent upon a number of factors, such as income distribution, tax structure, and the potential strength of the entrepreneurial strata. The government can influence the point of tangency through its monetary and fiscal policies, moving it down toward point A via progressive taxation and increased transfer payments or up toward point B by relying on regressive taxes.[10]

We can superimpose on Figure 3 the indifference-preference map ($I_g$) of the central planning board in a centrally planned economy. History suggests that the point of tangency, D, will lie between C and B, tending toward B in the early stages of planning on account of the drive for industrialization. This can be seen by comparing Yugoslavia and some other countries in Europe. In 1957 the Yugoslavs consumed 52 per cent of their social product. Comparably developed but market-oriented countries in Europe (Greece, Turkey, Spain, Portugal, Ireland, Southern Italy) consumed between 74 and 80 per cent of their GNP in that same year.[11] Assuming that the people of Yugoslavia are not more investment-conscious than the people in these other European countries, the conclusion seems to be self-evident: in Yugoslavia in 1957, point D was set above its potential consumer-directed level (i.e., above point C).

Where exactly point D will be set is decided by the central planning board, whose freedom of action is limited to the distance CB. The more industrialized the country becomes the more freedom the central planning board may have to impose its objectives and still assure the people of a slow but constant rise in the standard of living. And also, the more industrially developed a country is the less rational it becomes for the government to continue depressing consumption.

It may be argued that point D might be identical with point B, that is, the government plan may keep the standard of living at its lowest possible level. The argument is valid, and it may be true either in the early stages of industrialization or in an extremely underdeveloped country, such as China, where the distance AB is probably insignificant. However, this identity as a long-run proposition would involve an assumption of political irrationality because even the most totalitarian regime is not totally independent of the opinions of its populace. Point D may even be set above B, but it is clear that this could occur only for a very short period of time.

In summary, the division of the national product between consumption and investment in a centrally planned economy can vary between two limiting points: the minimum standard of living, whatever it happens to be in a particular country – and it certainly is not the same in China, the U.S.S.R., and Yugoslavia – and the point which would, in the absence of centrally imposed allocation of resources, be determined by market forces. The discretionary freedom of the government to administer the distribution of the national output between consumption and investment depends on the distance between these two points. The wider the distance between C and B, the easier it should be for the central planning board to satisfy both the planned goals and the pressure coming from the people for more consumption goods. Indications are that we are witnessing this development now in Yugoslavia and also in the U.S.S.R. For Yugoslavia such a trend has been suggested by the analysis of the pattern of organizational changes, and will be confirmed in the following chapters.

In the determination of the allocation of national income between consumption and investment, there seems to be no basic difference between the investment planning of Yugoslavia and the production planning of the U.S.S.R. In both systems of planning the central planning board determines, independently of the social scale of preferences, the aggregates concerning the supplies of consumer goods and investment goods. Yet it is necessary to stress the term *basic* difference. The Yugoslav Social Plan (which is an investment plan) leaves enough room for individual enterprises to modify point D by internal financing and credit creation by the communal banks. This is why point D in the Social Plan is stated in terms of anticipation. Another important point is that, unlike the Soviet model, the Yugoslav plan anticipates only the aggregate value of the investment component of national income and its distribution by industries, leaving it up to individual enterprises in each industry to determine the ultimate composition of output.

The second problem faced by a centrally planned economy is how to attain the most efficient use of resources so that the realized product coincides with point D on the $O_xO_y$ line (see Fig. 4).

It is likely that, for many different reasons, some misallocation of resources is inevitable in every economic system. And this misallocation would make for a divergence between potential and realized product, making points C and D fall inside the area $0O_xO_y$.

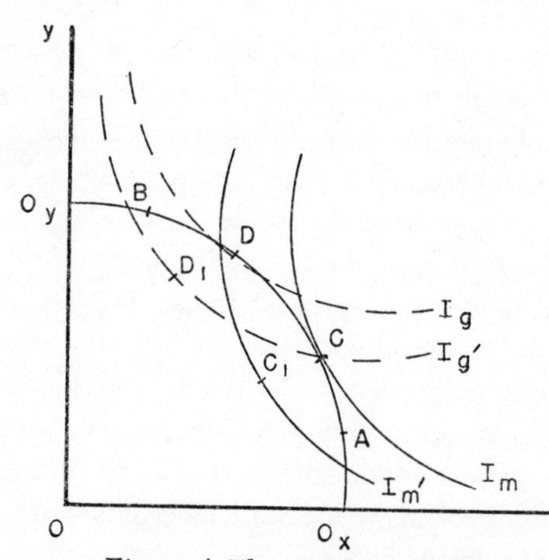


*Figure 4.* The problem of efficient utilization of resources.

This is true in capitalism, which has not been able as yet to solve the problem of cyclical unemployment and excess capacity of physical capital. If we assume that human wants are unlimited, no degree of "affluence" justifies this waste. In the West, various anticyclical and full-employment policies have been proposed and tried with different degrees of success to cope with this and similar problems.

Suppose that in a centrally planned economy the realized product is at $D_1$. It can be assumed that the problem of waste in a centrally planned economy is not one of getting resources employed but one of making their utilization most efficient once they are at work. Therefore, the main problem faced by the planned economy is to devise a strong system of incentives whose workings would push $D_1$ toward D. One should note in passing the major qualitative difference between underproduction in capitalism and in socialism. In capitalism the problem of waste of resources is the problem of unemployment. In socialism the problem of waste is the problem of inducing the agents of production to perform as efficiently as possible within the framework of technological knowledge.

In the Soviet model, the system of incentives is a combination of compulsion and material bonuses. Once point D is decided upon and resources allocated, the central planning board prescribes the production quotas expected of each enterprise, which in turn allocates quotas to each employee. For producing more than their quota, the workers and especially the managers receive money bonuses. They can do better than the established quota either because their quota was set too low, because they work harder, or because of a cost-saving innovation.

In Yugoslavia, since the early 1950's, the system of planning and with it the system of incentives has changed. The Yugoslav government decided that profit incentives were superior to the Soviet method of compulsion to meet planned quotas and material bonuses for overfulfilling the plan. The Yugoslav government relies on profit incentives to perform two important functions: (1) to improve the efficiency of the allocation of resources among direct producers, within the framework of the basic propositions of the Social Plan, and (2) to provide sufficient incentives to enterprises and their employees to maximize potential cost-saving innovations (through correlation between the profits of a firm and the wages paid to its employees).

The reliance on profit incentives raises an important problem: how to make some undertakings insisted upon by the government profitable. This is being done by various monetary and fiscal policies mentioned in Chapter I, such as price-fixing, taxes, and exemption from paying interest on the right of use. The evidence available, as well as my own observations, suggests that since the early 1950's the Yugoslav government has been using comprehensive economic measures to make some investments profitable (or unprofitable) rather than to order their financing through the federal budget.

Western authors have frequently said that the Yugoslav economy is a unique integration of Soviet and Western economic instruments. This may be a very misleading statement. It does not point out the real role played by market instruments in Yugoslavia. In fact, from the statement regarding the integration of two economic systems, one may almost conclude that it would be possible to draw a balance sheet from which we could judge from one year to another whether the Yugoslav economy has been becoming more pro-Western or pro-Soviet.

Although it is true that the Yugoslav economic system is a unique experiment which will have its place in comparative economic history, it is not entirely true that this system is an "integration" of the two major economic systems existing in today's world. The Yugoslav economy is a *centrally planned economy* and Yugoslavia is a *socialist* country. Whatever market instruments have been introduced into the system, the purpose of their introduction has been to find the best organization, to provide for most efficient allocation of resources, and to make people work harder without relying on direct compulsion, all in furtherance of the preconceived goal of socialism. The Yugoslav government uses various market instruments in order to make the Social Plan workable and efficient and to attain planned goals.* It is true, however, that the by-products of the ever-increasing scope of market instruments in Yugoslavia have been many and that the effects of them can be seen in a number of social, political, and economic institutions which emerged in the middle and late 1950's. Yet the increasing use of market criteria in the basic allocation

*One of the most prominent economic planners in Yugoslavia, the director of the Planning Commission for Croatia and as of Spring 1962 the vice-director of the Federal Planning Commission in Belgrade, wrote about the role of market in the Yugoslav economy: ". . . Market plays an important role in correcting the planned proportions of distribution and consumption, since it is precisely on the market that a direct check can be made as to whether these proportions have in fact been established in accordance with the action of economic laws and whether the measures necessary to enforce them have been taken" (see J. Sirotkovich, "Planned Economy of Yugoslavia," *Collective Economy of Yugoslavia* (Geneva: Geneva University Press, 1959), p. 140).

of resources does not mean a change in the socialist character of the country, unless one accepts the Marxian doctrine of the supremacy of the economic base and maintains that the use of market instruments inevitably transforms their users into ideological capitalists.

Finally, I shall make a brief comparison between India and Yugoslavia. Both countries rely on the investment plan for the allocation of resources among major macroeconomic variables, and it should be interesting, therefore, to note the differences between the initial allocation of resources in India's 1951–56 plan and the five-year Social Plan (1957–61) in Yugoslavia. Because of the different scope of different economic branches one cannot compare the distribution of the total investment fund in India and Yugoslavia. However, one may compare the initial allocation of resources in three basic economic branches:[12]

| | Percentage of Total Outlay | |
|---|---|---|
| | *Yugoslavia* | *India* |
| Industry | 44.0 | 8.4 |
| Agriculture | 19.1 | 17.5 |
| Transport and communications | 23.9 | 24.0 |

Yugoslav planning acknowledges the importance of man's will and of random elements in the process of economic development, and makes room for them by introducing market instruments and the criterion of profitability. Secondly, economic planning in Yugoslavia redelegates the problem of the allocation and use of resources within each industry to the direct producers and the banking system. These two are given sufficient incentives to work out the most efficient allocation and use of scarce resources possible within the framework of the Social Plan.

# III THE PERFORMANCE OF THE YUGOSLAV ECONOMY

THIS chapter will concentrate on the analysis of the performance of the Yugoslav economy as a whole, including the rate of economic growth since 1947, and on the analysis of some of the factors contributing to economic development. The ultimate aim of this chapter is to establish the relationship between the three major innovating actions of the Yugoslav government and the rate of economic growth.

## SOCIAL PRODUCT

Yugoslav statistics do not use the concept of national product. Their concept of *social product* covers the following economic activities: agriculture, mining, manufacturing, construction, transport, communications, trade, and catering. It leaves out as "unproductive services" such activities as state administration, personal services, the liberal professions, etc.,[1] but includes retail trade. The social product minus depreciation is *national income*. The social product is divided into the following basic categories: personal consumption, which includes expenditures on goods and services; general consumption, which includes expenditures on administration, education, defense, welfare, etc.; gross investment, which includes net investment and depreciation costs; the balance of exports and imports of goods and services; and finally "the increase of stocks which is entered into the difference together with differences in prices . . . and similar."[2]

A lively debate has developed in Yugoslavia recently on the meaning and scope of the concept of social product. Branko Horvat, one of the most qualified Yugoslav economists, seems to have initiated this debate when he was quoted as saying: "It is first necessary to define the purpose which the concept of social product is intended to serve; once this is done, the concept can be logically derived by means of a process that does not normally present much difficulty," and "The purpose of business is the satisfaction of human needs; more specifically, it consists in the achievement of economic welfare. . . . Economic welfare is everything that I regard as useful and desirable and that I would rather not be without."[3] Statements like this one are, of course, bound to cause a quick and vocal disagreement in a socialist state. The sharpest attack on Horvat's position came, to the best of my knowledge, from Ivan Friscich. Some of his remarks are: "Leaning heavily on this subjective judgment of the consumer, Horvat has, strictly speaking, betrayed his fundamental assumption that the purpose of business is the satisfaction of human needs. . . . Since social product is the problem at stake we cannot build our investigation on any implication that starts from an individual; we must build it only on those factors that stem from social considerations, which are the ones relevant for us. . . . The object of our attention cannot be personal consumption but rather social production."[4] It is hard to avoid the conclusion that Friscich's main thesis is that the government scale of preferences is superior to consumers' preferences. His statement, in fact, confirms the analysis in Chapter II, Figure 3 (p. 51).

Table 2. Social Product for the Period 1947–63, 1956 Prices (in Billions of Dinars)

| Year | Total | Year | Total |
|---|---|---|---|
| 1947 | 1,057 | 1956 | 1,612 |
| 1948 | 1,299 | 1957 | 1,982 |
| 1949 | 1,391 | 1958 | 2,025 |
| 1950 | 1,258 | 1959 | 2,373 |
| 1951 | 1,368 | 1960 | 2,519 |
| 1952 | 1,165 | 1961 | 2,670 |
| 1953 | 1,389 | 1962 | 2,777 |
| 1954 | 1,434 | 1963 | 3,110 |
| 1955 | 1,617 | 1964 | 3,421 |

SOURCE: *Statisticki Godisnjak* (Belgrade: Savezni Zarod za Statistiku, 1961), p. 99; *Politika*, April 8, 1962, and December 21, 1963; *Statistical Pocketbook*, 1965, p. 39.

Table 2 shows the quantitative performance of the Yugoslav economy in the postwar period. The initial high rate of growth lost its impetus in 1949, and the value of output attained in 1949 was not regained until 1953–54.

Industrial production has been in the forefront of Yugoslav planning since 1947 (Table 3) and the process of industrialization has continued throughout the postwar period. From the behavior of the agricultural component of output it appears that the process of industrialization was "forced" before the normal preconditions for the industrial development of an agrarian country were met, i.e., before the productivity of labor in

Table 3. Industrial Production [a]

| Year | Index | Year | Index |
|---|---|---|---|
| 1939 | 100 | 1955 | 242 |
| 1946 | 79 | 1956 | 266 |
| 1947 | 121 | 1957 | 311 |
| 1948 | 151 | 1958 | 345 |
| 1949 | 167 | 1959 | 391 |
| 1950 | 172 | 1960 | 451 |
| 1951 | 166 | 1961 | 483 |
| 1952 | 164 | 1962 | 516 |
| 1953 | 183 | 1963 | 596 |
| 1954 | 208 | 1964 | 691 |

SOURCE: *Statistical Pocketbook*, 1963, p. 49, and *ibid.*, 1965, p. 51.

[a] A few numerical examples indicate the extent of the industrial development of Yugoslavia: kilowatt-hours of electrical energy produced in 1939, 1,173,000,000, in 1960, 8,928,000,000; tons of coal produced in 1939, 7,032,000, in 1960, 22,713,000; tons of crude petroleum produced in 1939, 1,000, in 1960, 944,000; tons of steel produced in 1939, 235,000, in 1960, 1,442,000; number of cars manufactured in 1939, none, in 1960, 10,461; number of radios manufactured in 1939, none, in 1960, 239,000,000; tons of cotton yarn manufactured in 1939, 19,000, in 1960, 51,000; pairs of leather footwear manufactured in 1939, 4,200,000, in 1960, 15,000,000 (*Statistical Pocketbook*, 1961, pp. 46–49).

Table 4. Agricultural Production [a]
(1930–39 = 100)

| Year | Index | Year | Index |
|---|---|---|---|
| 1947 | 89 | 1955 | 116 |
| 1948 | 103 | 1956 | 97 |
| 1949 | 103 | 1957 | 140 |
| 1950 | 75 | 1958 | 124 |
| 1951 | 106 | 1959 | 163 |
| 1952 | 75 | 1960 | 146 |
| 1953 | 106 | 1961 | 141 |
| 1954 | 94 | 1962 | 142 |

SOURCE: *Statisticki Godisnjak*, 1962, p. 107, and *Statistical Pocketbook*, 1961, p. 40.

[a] Here are a few examples, all in thousands of tons: wheat in 1930–39, 2,430, in 1960, 3,570; rye in 1930–39, 212, in 1960, 233; hemp in 1930–39, 250, in 1960, 200; potatoes in 1930–39, 1,650, in 1960, 3,160; plums in 1930–39, 505, in 1960, 208; maize in 1930–39, 4,300, in 1960, 6,120 (*Statistical Pocketbook*, 1961, p. 37).

agriculture (see Table 4) had increased sufficiently to create surpluses in population as well as in the quantity of food produced.*

The First Five Year Plan was a complete failure. It "ordered" production to increase 2½ times in 1951 over that in 1939. However, as Table 3 shows, industrial production in 1951 was only 66 per cent over that in 1939, and not until the end of 1955 had it reached the rate planned for 1951. A number of reasons were voiced to explain this failure of the First Five Year Plan. The Yugoslavs themselves attributed the failure of their first plan to two factors: the Cominform blockade, and the bureaucratic control of the economy. The Cominform blockade was blamed because the bulk of the Yugoslav trade was at that time with the East and the sudden cut in trade meant a serious blow to the Yugoslav economy. Since this experience the Yugoslavs have been very cautious in trading with the Soviet bloc. Two years after the 1955 Tito-Khrushchev reconciliation in Belgrade, one of the leading Yugoslav economic periodicals complained about trade relationships with the Soviet bloc. This time the problem arose from the Soviet pressure to conclude long-range trade agreements calling for exact specifications of the quality and quantity of exports and imports. It was impossible for the Yugoslavs to accept any such agreements as these because of the nature of the new Yugoslav economic system.[5]

The failure of the first economic plan may be laid to a single cause: no man or group of men can set up a rigid and at the same time workable framework of actions and activities either for themselves or for their fellowmen. It is impossible to predict man's behavior with mathematical exactness, and any attempt to regiment his behavior must lead either to

*Stjepan Han made an interesting comparison of the productivity of work in agriculture in different countries. The calculation is done in thousands of units per man.

| | *1934–38* | *1948–52* | *1959* |
|---|---|---|---|
| India | 1.1 | 1.4 | 1.5 |
| Turkey | 1.6 | 2.5 | 2.2 |
| Greece | 4.1 | 3.9 | 4.6 |
| Yugoslavia | 2.2 | 2.1 | 2.5 |
| Poland | 3.5 | 4.4 | 4.2 |
| United States | 20.9 | 43.4 | 45.8 |
| France | 11.6 | 9.3 | 12.7 |
| Canada | 22.3 | 35.2 | 33.4 |
| West Germany | 14.9 | 13.3 | 12.7 |

See Ing. Stjepan Han, *Sustina, Znaca i Faktori Productivnosti Rada* (Belgrade: 1959), p. 17.

complete failure as in Yugoslavia, or to the flourishing of black market activities such as occur in the U.S.S.R.,[6] and ultimately to the degeneration of man, as Maritain pointed out.[7] Black market activities can be considered as a protest against the attempt to regiment the behavior of the members of a society.

The analysis of the correlation between the pattern of organizational changes already described and the rate of economic growth suggests an interesting relation: as the rate of growth declined after 1949, the Yugoslav government reacted by introducing an organizational innovation which took place *de jure* in 1950–51, and *de facto* in 1953.* When in economic trouble, the Yugoslav government acted as an innovator, trying to find a better socioeconomic organization. Its anticyclical policies did not aim at improving the level of economic activity from within the economic system. The government changed the system itself.

The rate of growth declined in 1961 and the Yugoslav government preferred – once again – a qualitative change in the organization of its economy to more conventional quantitative anticyclical policies. The following years witnessed *de facto* implementation of the structural innovation of 1961, and the rate of growth rose from 6 per cent in 1961 and 4 per cent in 1962 to 12 per cent in 1963, and was approximately 10 per cent in 1964.[8]

## INFLATION

The problem of inflation in Yugoslavia appeared as soon as the organizational innovation of 1950–51 had begun to be implemented, that is, sometime in 1953. In the period 1953–61, prices rose, on the average, 5.72 per cent a year.[9] During the first four months of 1962, retail prices increased by approximately 25 per cent and the prices of agricultural products rose by 18 per cent.[10] This galloping inflation was checked in the last part of 1962, and the price level rose by 6 per cent in 1963 and 5

*For most foreign writers *de jure* and *de facto* turning points of the Yugoslav economy as it diverged from the Soviet model are identical and date back to 1950–51. From this misunderstanding of the true relationship between the major declarative laws such as the one on planned management of the national economy of 1951, and the subsequent operational laws, stems their assertion that operational laws are a kind of retreat from the market economy. They missed the point here; without the clarifying operational laws there would be no practical value in the major declarative acts. As an example, see John M. Montias, "Economic Reform and Retreat in Yugoslavia," *Foreign Affairs,* January 1959. The retreats mentioned by Montias were in fact attempts to make the new economic system operational, and those "retreats" set the stage for still another, more progressive, organizational innovation in 1961.

per cent in 1964.[11] In the summer of 1965 still another hyperinflation took place, sending the price level up by about 30 per cent. Any analysis of rising prices in Yugoslavia must distinguish between continuous creeping inflation and the hyperinflations of 1962 and 1965.

The Social Plan anticipates creeping inflation—for 1962 the Social Plan envisaged a 5 per cent increase in the price level. The mildness of the monetary measures against inflation suggests that Yugoslav planners have realized the inevitability of some inflation in a developing economy. The rise of the institution of profit in Yugoslavia provided incentives to produce new and better goods, which in turn pushed prices up. Bidding for skilled labor (a very scarce commodity in Yugoslavia) raised the prices of

Table 5. Money Supply, 1952–61

| Year | Total Money Supply[a] | Percentage of Change |
|---|---|---|
| 1952 | 320 | ... |
| 1955 | 410 | 28 |
| 1958 | 721 | 76 |
| 1961 | 1,252 | 74 |

SOURCE: M. Vuckovich, "The Recent Development of the Money and Banking System of Yugoslavia," *Journal of Political Economy*, August 1963, p. 368.
[a] In billions of dinars.

innovating products by increasing costs. Higher money wages, more liberal policies with respect to consumer credits, and the ability of communal banks to extend short-term credits* contributed to higher prices by increasing demand. At the same time the real degree of this creeping inflation may have been exaggerated. A developing economy like Yugoslavia's experiences continuous injection of new goods into the stream of economic life. The introduction of these new goods means the creation of new wants and a complete and continuous reshaping of consumers' preferences in favor of new, better, and higher-priced goods. The acceptance of creeping inflation by the Yugoslav government as a more efficient alternative to the Soviet type of administrative economic development is suggested by its liberal policy with respect to the rate of growth in the supply of money (see Table 5).

*Short-term bank credits increased from 714 billion dinars in 1952 to 1,049 billion in 1955, 1,329 billion in 1958, and 2,061 billion in 1961 (see M. Vuckovich, "The Recent Development of the Money and Banking System of Yugoslavia," *Journal of Political Economy*, August 1963, p. 368).

While the supply of money had to grow to finance the rate of growth in real output, the rate of change in the supply of money went beyond this requirement, thus allowing also for intra- and interindustrial bidding for scarce resources and contributing in this manner both to inflation and to an economic development characterized by ever-changing composition of output.

The hyperinflation of 1962 was triggered by the simultaneous action of a number of factors. The following contributing factors were most frequently mentioned: (1) New rate of exchange. In January 1961, an agreement with the International Monetary Fund was reached to devaluate the dinar from 300 to the dollar to 750. (2) New goods. To avoid price controls, enterprises had only to change their products (very slightly) and to demonstrate to the price authorities the high cost of producing "new goods." (3) The wrong application of price controls. More often than not wholesale prices were controlled while retail prices were not. In 1961, retail prices of almost all consumer goods were freed from administrative controls and retail stores immediately cashed in their involuntarily accumulated "unliquidated" (monopoly) gain. This thesis is supported by the fact that between December 1961 and the end of April 1962 the wholesale price level of industrial products rose by 2 per cent, while retail prices increased by 25 per cent. (4) Pressure of wage increases. After the Law on the Distribution of the Total Revenue of Enterprises of 1961 was enacted, wages rose by 8.7 per cent while the rate of productivity increased by 6.1 per cent.

Each of these factors had some marginal influence on inflation in 1962; no one of them was both the sufficient and necessary cause of this inflation. To understand the inflation of 1962 it is necessary to combine all these factors and view them in the light of the organizational framework of the Yugoslav economy.

In 1961 the Workers' Councils were allowed to distribute net profits between the wage bill and internal funds in accordance with their own preferences. The outcome, as we have just seen, was an increase in wages (8.7 per cent) in excess of the rate of productivity improvement (6.1 per cent). After allocating a greater share of net profits to the wage bill, the enterprises had to increase their demands for credit from the banks. This is a reasonable inference, because in the second half of 1961 and the beginning of 1962 the economy continued to grow and generate expanding needs for production funds, even though there was a considerable slowdown in the rate of growth (from 12 per cent in 1960 to 7 per cent in 1961 and to 4 per cent in 1962).

The important question here is, Did the local banks have funds and authority to grant credits to the enterprises? Yes, they did. The General Investment Fund in its total size as well as in its allocation among individual industries in the economy is predetermined by the Social Plan. As individual firms receive their competitively allocated investment loans from corresponding specialized banks these funds, as they are drawn upon, will find their way into local communal banks.

The communal banks are required by law to hold 30 per cent of all their deposits as reserves with the National Bank, and can lend out the rest as short-term credits. Since a given sum may be lent out, repaid, and lent out again, it follows that the total amount of bank credits extended in any one year may exceed the total amount anticipated in the Social Plan. The size of the excess in a given period of time will be larger the faster the short-term credits are repaid.

In fact, the Yugoslav government moved in swiftly and excessive inflation was checked in the second half of 1962. Two major actions of the government were: (1) a guideline for the distribution of net profits between the wage bill and internal funds (see Ch. I, p. 31); and (2) an increase in the number of price-controlled "strategic" goods.

The ability of the banks to extend short-term credits supports inflationary pressures in the sense that short-term credits make it possible for firms to bid for resources and continue a high level of profit-oriented investment activity. For example, here is an index of short-term credits: 1959 ÷ 1958, 120; 1960 ÷ 1959, 114; 1961 ÷ 1960, 115; 1962 ÷ 1961, 111; 1963 ÷ 1962, 123 (*Statisticki Godisnjak*, 1964, p. 279).

The hyperinflation of 1965 should be viewed as a corrective and welcome measure of the Yugoslav government. In the early 1960's, as we have seen in Chapter I, consumer goods were sold at prices equal to their costs plus "planned" profit. At the same time, the prices of raw material and intermediate products were not allowed to respond to changes in consumers' preferences without previous approval by the government. The results were repressed inflation, distorted relative prices, overdevelopment of consumer-goods industries with respect to the availability of raw materials and intermediate products (but not necessarily with respect to consumers' demand), and the consequent misallocation of investment funds in favor of finished-goods producers. By lifting its controls over the prices of raw materials and intermediate goods the Yugoslav government underwrote price increases. The industries producing raw materials and intermediate products were allowed to increase their prices in order to eliminate the excess demand for their products. This, in turn, makes them more profitable and increases their investment activity. At the same time, consumer-goods industries had to raise their prices to maintain the "planned" rate of profit. It is to be expected, however, that the 1965 inflation will cut down on the aggregate demand for consumer goods. Thus, an increase in unused capacities in some sectors of the economy, reflecting the misallocation of resources caused by price regulations, should come as no surprise. This is why the 1965 inflation was a welcome and positive measure of the Yugoslav government. Its main aim was to establish relative prices more consistent with true consumers' preferences and to improve, consequently, the flow of investment funds.

The Yugoslav analyses of the problem of rising prices are somewhat confusing and often contradictory. Professor Vuckovich, for example, first admits that the mounting inflationary pressures were owing to a fast rise in the supply of money and that "the main and almost sole reason for the increase in the supply of money was the expansion in the volume of short-term credits with all banks." [12] But in the same study, he states that ". . . banks cannot determine freely the volume of credits and money. They cannot influence the size of the money supply . . . the amount of new credits is determined every year by the federal social plan." [13]

Vuckovich also maintains that an unfavorable balance of payments has exercised upward pressure on the price level in Yugoslavia. If Yugoslav exports and imports were administratively planned as in the U.S.S.R. we could infer from this statement that Yugoslavia exports consumer goods and imports only means of production. Statistics, however, rule this out. And his "remedy": by *higher tariffs on imports* he proposes to fight inflation by *restricting* the supply of goods and services! A very doubtful remedy indeed.

## THE RATE AND PATTERN OF INVESTMENT

In 1952 the Yugoslav plan changed its content and became an investment-oriented plan which only anticipates the magnitude and composition of the Social Product. The Yugoslav government was forced into the language of "anticipations" by the very economic system it itself had created. The government does not know in advance how many enterprises will compete for investment funds and what kinds of products they will turn out.

The realization of the Yugoslav planners that any attempt to impose a deterministic system is detrimental to the national economy and may, consequently, be eventually detrimental to the regime itself, was voiced by Edvard Kardelj, vice-president in the Yugoslav government, who said in his Oslo address in 1954: "The Yugoslav system of self-management of the economy is based on two fundamental assumptions: no central leadership can control the entire economic and social development of the country. The second is that the maximum effort and initiative of the individual does not depend so much upon directives and control as it does upon the personal economic, social, cultural and material interests of the worker. To ignore either assumption automatically leads to bureaucratic despotism." [14]

Before the analysis of the actual rate of investment, a short comment on the potential rationality of investment decisions in a centrally planned economy is appropriate. It will be recalled that the text of the Social Plan for 1962 included specific remarks about shortcomings which had appeared in the Social Plan for 1961. As Oskar Lange pointed out, planning authorities gain new experience every year, and from one year to another they can apply the same system of trial and error that we do in the West, with the advantage that they can coordinate the whole economy.[15] The Yugoslav economic system supports this thesis. Since Yugoslav enterprises operate for profit, from their income statements the government can derive information about the structure of the aggregate demand and allocate investment funds in accordance with consumers' preferences. Therefore, on an a priori ground there is no reason to assume that economic planners in Yugoslavia cannot possess all data necessary for the rational allocation of investment funds — provided that we agree to identify the concept of economic rationality with the satisfaction of consumers' preferences constrained by the prevailing income distribution.

The rate of investment in Yugoslavia has been both high and stable as a percentage of the social product; this is illustrated by the figures in Tables 6 and 7.

The argument used by Yugoslav economists to justify this high rate of investment is — besides, as they point out, the fact that Yugoslavia wants to become an industrialized country — that investment expenditures regulate employment. And, in their opinion, the availability of jobs to all those willing to work is the *first* duty of the economy. Branko Horvat has said that the optimum rate of investment is a function of the human factor.[16] Professor Djordje Misich wrote that the minimum investment

Table 6. Investments in Industry and Agriculture (in Millions of Dinars)

| Year | Industry and Mining | Agriculture and Forestry |
|---|---|---|
| 1954 | 195,250 | 20,496 |
| 1955 | 205,375 | 31,843 |
| 1956 | 184,748 | 44,088 |
| 1957 | 178,459 | 60,252 |
| 1958 | 177,350 | 78,908 |
| 1959 | 223,895 | 121,441 |
| 1960 | 310,668 | 118,450 |
| 1961 | 408,689 | 118,906 |
| 1962 | 447,846 | 136,594 |
| 1963 | 532,217 | 157,329 |

SOURCE: *Statisticki Godisnjak*, 1960, p. 233; *ibid.*, 1962, p. 228; and *ibid.*, 1964, p. 272.

Table 7. Gross Investment as a Percentage of Social Product

| Year | Social Product[a] | Gross Investment[a] | Gross Investment/ Social Product[b] |
|---|---|---|---|
| 1953 | 1,134 | 363 | 34.7 |
| 1954 | 1,299 | 423 | 32.6 |
| 1955 | 1,552 | 449 | 28.9 |
| 1956 | 1,612 | 461 | 28.6 |
| 1957 | 1,891 | 550 | 29.1 |
| 1958 | 1,987 | 587 | 29.5 |
| 1959 | 2,404 | 702 | 29.2 |
| 1960 | 2,959 | 879 | 29.7 |

SOURCE: *Yearbook of National Accounts Statistics, 1960* (New York: United Nations, 1961) pp. 244–247.
[a] In billions of current dinars.
[b] As percentage.

is determined by the rate of change in the labor force while the maximum investment is determined by the existing distribution of the social product between consumption and investment, since neither Yugoslavia nor any other country would be willing to lower the percentage of its gross national product going into consumption.[17] The rate of consumption has shown a significant degree of stability as a percentage of the social product; between 1953 and 1964 personal consumption ranged between 51 and 55 per cent of the social product.[18] Comparing this stable share with the growth of the social product (see Table 2) reveals that the level of consumption has increased absolutely from year to year since 1953.

The analyses of Horvat and Misich and the fact that the capital-output ratio in some industries for which large investment sums have been allocated is as high as 5.2 explain why the full employment rate of investment is so high in Yugoslavia.

Since the innovation of 1950–51 and its implementation in and after 1953, the role of internal financing, which is not directly restrained by the basic propositions of the Social Plan, has increased. The Law on Investment Loans of July 25, 1956, introduced a provision whereby the enterprise asking a loan must help to finance the project from its own funds. In this way internal funds, by financing the project in part, are channeled, willingly or not, in accordance with the basic propositions of the plan. The scope of internal financing has increased since 1956, when it amounted to 16 per cent of gross investment, to over 30 per cent in 1963.

The pattern of investment activity in Yugoslavia has been shifting from capital goods industries toward consumer goods industries, including agriculture, ever since the *de facto* change in the system of planning in 1953. In manufacturing and mining the gross fixed investment, which had been 61 per cent of the total of gross fixed investment in the period 1952–57, declined to 36 per cent in the period 1957–59; its percentage of the social product declined between the same time periods from 18 to 9. Meanwhile the gross fixed investment in agriculture and forestry, which had been 6 per cent of the total of gross fixed investment in 1950–53, increased to 13 per cent in 1954–59, and as a percentage of the steadily increasing social product it rose from 2 to 3.5. The accompanying tabulation shows the shift toward the manufacture of goods for consumption; the figures are the investment in different industries as percentages of the total gross fixed investment in manufacturing.

| *Industry* | *1952–53* | *1957–58* |
|---|---|---|
| Metals (using) | 32 | 18 |
| Metals (making) | 21 | 17 |
| Chemicals | 13 | 12 |
| Food, beverages, tobacco | 6 | 16 |
| Textiles | 4 | 9 |
| Other goods | 24 | 28 |

Table 8 shows the increased place of internal financing in investment.

Three factors contributed to this shift in the pattern of investment: the increased scope of internal financing, which is presumably profit-oriented and relatively free from the constraints of the basic propositions of the Social Plan; pressures coming from the workers, whose earnings depend on the profitability of the enterprises employing them in turn depends on consumers' preferences subject to the income distribution constraint; and the monetary and fiscal policies of the Yugoslav government.

Table 8. Sources of Gross Investment for 1953 and 1960

| Sources | 1953 [a] | Percentage | 1960 [a] | Percentage |
|---|---|---|---|---|
| Autonomous investment [b] | 213,405 | 62.7 | 465,944 | 52.9 |
| Internal financing | 37,093 | 10.9 | 182,691 | 20.8 |
| Depreciation | 74,529 | 21.8 | 145,175 | 16.3 |
| Other social funds | 14,652 | 4.3 | 50,189 | 5.7 |
| Total [c] | 340,622 | 100 | 879,450 | 100 |

SOURCE: Data in *Statisticki Godisnjak*, 1956 and 1961.

[a] In millions of dinars.

[b] General Investment Fund, investment funds of People's Republics, and local governments.

[c] Including investments financed through Budgets.

While the impact of the first two factors on the pattern of investment is self-evident, the Yugoslav monetary and fiscal policies must be subjected to economic analysis in order to assess the government's intentions.

In the beginning of 1954 and for about two years thereafter the competitive rate of interest (described fully p. 20) played an important overall role in the allocation of investment funds for different uses within each industry. To discover the real impact of the competitive rate of interest on the pattern of investment, let us observe two firms in the same industry, one capital-intensive and the other labor-intensive, operating under identical conditions. By identical conditions we shall mean identical production functions ($X = L^{1/2}, C^{1/2}$), the elasticity of substitution of factors of production as equal to one, and approximately uniform expected average total wage rates.*

If these two firms were competing for the same investment funds and were expecting (given the assumptions) similar rates of return on capital invested, which could offer a higher interest? The assumptions concern-

*It will be recalled from Chapter I that in the period 1954–61 total wages consisted of two parts: the basic wage and additional income paid from profits.

ing identical operating conditions are needed in order to ascertain the real impact of competitive bidding on the pattern of investment.

The rate of interest a firm can afford to pay depends on the ratio of net profits (NP) to net investment (Inv). Since net profits consisted (before 1961) of additional pay to the workers ($W_e$, where e equals extra) and internal funds (I), the ratio NP/Inv can be rewritten as $(W_e + I)/Inv$.

With few exceptions, loans are repaid from the internal funds of a firm. This makes the ratio of additional payments to internal funds ($W_e/I$) crucial in determining the ability of the firm to pay interest.

This ratio is closely related to the ratio of capital to labor. Graphically, the function slopes downward to the right, indicating a negative correlation between the ratio of additional payments to internal funds and the ratio of capital to labor. That is, a firm that has a high ratio of capital goods to labor can afford to pay its workers some additional wages and still have a comparatively low ratio of these payments to internal funds; machines don't share in the extra wages. On the other hand, a labor-intensive firm will find that this wage fund is high relative to internal funds. The greater this ratio, the less the firm can afford to pay for its investment funds, given the expected rate of return.

The capital-intensive firm, other things being equal, would have a definite advantage over the labor-intensive firm in competition for investment funds.

The high expectations for the system in which the competitive rate of interest was the allocator of funds among competing uses within the same industrial branch (not between different branches since the elasticity of substitution of investment funds between different branches is close to zero because of the rigidity of planned proportions) turned to bitter disappointment. As we saw in Chapter I, in order to get loans, enterprises offered extremely high rates of interest, in the hope that the marginal rate would be lower than the one they offered – once the marginal rate was established, all successful applicants paid only the marginal rate. They hoped that by offering a higher rate of interest than they could reasonably afford to pay their applications had a better chance of being intramarginal. Since this behavior was more or less common among all enterprises, the result was that the marginal rate of interest was getting high relative to the expected net returns. Finally, in March 1955, the government gave up the institution of competitive rates of interest and in the subsequent years the importance of the competitive rate of interest diminished. In March

1961 the competitive rate of interest as an allocator of investment funds disappeared almost altogether.

Professor Neuberger [19] has suggested that one reason for the lack of success of this instrument of investment control was the absence of a price system with a high degree of rationality. His argument is that the competitive rate of interest manifested the preferences of planners for distributing investment funds through the cost curves of enterprises. However, Neuberger maintains, the Yugoslav price system is not suitable for allocating resources according to social opportunity costs. Professor Neuberger in fact asserts that Yugoslav prices are not consistent with the planners' preferences. There is no doubt that the outcome of competitive bidding in Yugoslavia had to be different from that in a free market economy. Yet, given the government scale of preferences and the price systems serving it, there is no ground for asserting that competitive bidding for funds could not distribute investment goods in accordance with the profitability of different projects – at the same time rendering the price system consistent with planners' preferences (or indicating miscalculations). Those projects whose selling prices were fixed substantially below or above their profit-maximizing levels would be out of the competition while others whose selling prices were fixed close to their potential market levels would stand a good chance of getting loans.

The competitive rate of interest seems to be a good objective criterion for the allocation of scarce resources in a developing economy, when the government acts as the major entrepreneur. Probably the main reason this instrument failed in Yugoslavia was the lack of ability of the banking system to enforce its proper use. The Law on Loans for Commercial Investments from the G.I.F. of January 28, 1954, gave the banks both the right and the duty to reject all financially unsound projects. If the banks had carefully considered each application for a loan and rejected all applicants who offered rates in excess of the potential marginal efficiency of their investment projects, the instrument of competitive rate of interest could have been successfully maintained.

Had the competitive rate of interest continued to exist through 1957, the Law on the Cancellation of Contracts for Loans from the G.I.F. of February 6, 1957 (see Ch. I, p. 18), would have introduced some significant modifications in the results of competitive bidding. The effect of this law would have been to narrow the gap between planners' and consumers' preferences. As of February 1957 capital-intensive projects would have had to be consumer-oriented to become eligible for competition for investment funds.

After 1961, the role of taxation policy with respect to the investment behavior of the Yugoslav firm increased in importance.

Let us start the analysis of the relationship between the taxation policy of the government and the investment behavior of the firm with the 1961 scheme of the distribution of the gross profits of the firm (see Ch. I, p. 31).

First, a federal tax ($T_f$) of 15 per cent of gross profit ($P_g$) of the firm is paid, yielding net profit ($P_n$):

$$T_f = .15\,P_g, \text{ and} \quad (1)$$

$$P_n = .85\,P_g. \quad (2)$$

Second, the internal funds of the firm (I) are deducted from the net profit, yielding the total wage bill (W):

$$W + I = P_n = .85\,P_g. \quad (3)$$

Third, the wage fund is subject to a 15 per cent tax to the local government ($T_w$), while internal funds (excluding the reserve fund) are subject to a 20 per cent tax ($T_i$) to the local government. Assuming that $\Delta$ reserve fund = 0, then

$$T_w = .15W, \text{ and } T_i = .20I.$$

Since $T_f = .15P_g$, $T_w = .15W$, and $T_i = 20I$, and $T_{total} = T_f + T_w + T_i$, then

$$T_t = .15P_g + .15W + .20I.$$

Since $W + I = .85P_g$, then

$$T_t = .15P_g + .15(.85P_g - I) + .20I,$$

$$T_t = .2775P_g + .05I, \text{ or} \quad (4)$$

$$T_t = .15P_g + .15W + .20(.85P_g - W),$$

$$T_t = .32P_g - .05W. \quad (5)$$

Finally the average marginal tax rate emerges:

$$T_t/P_g = .2775 + .05(I/P_g), \text{ or} \quad (6)$$

$$T_t/P_g = .32 - .05(W/P_g). \quad (7)$$

From (6) and (7) we can see that an increase in the ratio of the wage bill to internal funds (W/I) would (as long as $P_n = W + I$) increase the $W/P_g$ ratio and decrease the percentage of tax paid. Then two crucial questions become (1) how can the firm increase the W/I ratio? and (2) what are the consequences of an increase in the ratio of the wage bill to internal funds?

The wage bill (W) of the Yugoslav firm is: $W = P_g - .15P_g - I$, or $W = P_n - I$.

The firm is supposed to solve the problem of distribution of its net profits between internal funds and payroll, as we saw in Chapter I, by using the following guideline:

$$W = P_n/(1 + XY) \qquad (8)$$

where X equals the ratio of internal funds to wage bill ($X = I/W$) and is calculated for each year ($X_1$) on the basis of data from the previous year ($X_0$) in the following manner:

$$X_1 = (K_1/K_0)X_0, \qquad (9)$$

where K equals capital per worker. Since $X = I/W$, Equation 9 can be written as

$$(I/W)_1 = (K_1/K_0) \times (I/W)_0.$$

The variable Y in Equation 8 we can call the productivity coefficient. If an increase in the net profits ($P_n$) of the firm comes about from a price increase, the productivity coefficient in (8) must be adjusted so that W does not change, i.e., so that all extra profits are allocated to the internal funds of the firm. If, on the other hand, higher profits come from productivity improvements, the productivity coefficient must be calculated so that extra profit is allocated to the wage bill.

From the wage determination guideline (8) it appears that two avenues are open to the firm in order to increase its W/I ratio: to increase $P_n$, with X and Y in (8) remaining constant, and/or to decrease X. In either case, the percentage of net profit allocated to the wage bill would rise.

Let us examine both courses. 1. Given the size of the firm, its net profits can be increased either (a) because the demand curve becomes more inelastic (i.e., via price increases) or (b) via productivity improvements. In case (a) coefficient Y in (8) would increase so that $\Delta W = 0$ and $\Delta I = \Delta P_n$. In case (b) the productivity coefficient Y would be calculated so that $\Delta W = \Delta P_n$. This is how the Yugoslav government has built into the economic system an incentive to raise the ratio of output per man.

2. Another way to increase the wage bill as a percentage of net profits of the firm is suggested in Equations 8 and 9. X in (8) can be decreased by a decline in the ratio of capital to labor. And the capital-labor ratio will decrease if the ratio of the investment in variable capital (labor) to net investment is greater than the ratio of the investment in fixed capital

to net investment—which means that labor-intensive investments, by changing the ratio of wage bill to internal funds, tend to lower the ratio of total tax to gross profit.

The expected effects of the taxation policy after 1961 seem to be rather different from those of the system of competitive bidding of December 1953. Although the system of competitive bidding tended to encourage capital-intensive projects, the subsequent tax policy encourages labor-intensive projects. The reasons for this change are many: increase in unemployment; accelerated migration of peasants to the cities (approximately 100,000 a year); more attention paid to export industries (Yugoslavia should have comparative advantage, in relation to the West, in the production of labor-intensive goods).

The final consideration with respect to the pattern of investment is that of marginal capital-output ratio. Marginal capital-output ratio is usually defined as the ratio of gross fixed investment to increase in output. *The Economic Survey of Europe* [20] gives the marginal capital-output ratio for Yugoslavia as 3.5 in the period 1948–59. For the period 1952–58 the ratio is 2.2, with the following breakdown by industrial branches: food, beverages, and tobacco, 1.1; metal-making, 5.2; textiles and clothing, 0.8; metal-using, 1.2; and chemicals, 3.4.

Marginal capital-output ratio taken by itself does not say much. A decline in this ratio can mean increased productivity, but it can also mean a switch in the pattern of investment from capital-intensive to labor-intensive industries. Judging from the analysis in this chapter it seems that the declining marginal capital-output ratio in Yugoslavia is explainable by the shift in the pattern of investment activity.[21]

The analysis of the rate and pattern of investment activity in Yugoslavia has indicated that the persistently high rate of investment transformed itself into a high rate of growth only after 1953, i.e., after the innovation of 1950–51, which called for a change in the pattern of investment, was implemented. The high and constant rate of investment was, in fact, insufficient to maintain a steady rate of growth. The Yugoslav experience is an interesting confirmation of the Schumpeter theory of economic development. Writing twenty-five years before Keynes proposed to cure economic stagnation by quantitative changes in the rate of investment, Schumpeter said — and explained analytically in his *Theory* and later in his *Business Cycles* empirically — that only qualitative changes in the pattern of investment can bring about economic growth. A change in the pattern of investment means a new production function, which in turn calls for a change in organization. This is why innovation is not only the engine of economic development but is also a cause of social reorganization.

## THE LABOR FORCE

Statistical data on the labor force in Yugoslavia (Table 9) show a relatively fast increase in the number of people employed.

Table 9. Employment in Yugoslavia

| Occupation | 1956 | 1958 | 1960 | 1962 |
|---|---|---|---|---|
| Industry | 800,900 | 995,100 | 1,130,000 | 1,181,000 |
| Construction | 233,900 | 252,000 | 294,100 | 331,000 |
| Trade | 206,700 | 221,800 | 258,800 | 324,000 |
| Total[a] | 2,320,900 | 2,637,300 | 3,069,100 | 3,419,000 |

SOURCE: *Statisticki Godisnjak*, 1962, p. 82, and *Statistical Pocketbook*, 1963, pp. 30–31, for the 1962 figures.
[a] Including other occupations but not private farmers.

At the same time the number of unemployed workers has also been increasing, as Table 10 reveals. Unemployment is not a typical feature of socialist economies, and even more surprising is the matter-of-fact treatment of this problem in Yugoslav statistics. Unemployed workers, in general, are unskilled blue-collar workers coming to the cities from their overcrowded farms. An average of 100,000 peasants move to the cities each year.[22] It will be recalled that this flight of peasants into the cities was one of the sources of labor supply in Western economies in the

Table 10. Unemployment in Yugoslavia (in Thousands)

| Unemployed | 1957 | 1958 | 1959 | 1960 | 1961 | 1962 | 1963 |
|---|---|---|---|---|---|---|---|
| Blue-collar workers | 115.3 | 163.7 | 154.5 | 175.0 | 221.1 | 253.7 | 207.3 |
| Unskilled | 98.8 | 139.7 | 133.9 | 154.5 | 189.2 | 210.3 | 175.8 |
| Skilled | 16.5 | 24.0 | 20.6 | 20.5 | 31.9 | 43.4 | 31.5 |
| White-collar workers | 8.4 | 10.0 | 10.0 | 9.9 | 11.5 | 20.3 | 21.7 |
| Without high-school degree | 7.3 | 8.5 | 8.4 | 8.4 | 8.8 | 14.1 | 14.0 |
| High-school degree or equivalent | 1.0 | 1.3 | 1.4 | 1.3 | 2.3 | 5.2 | 6.5 |
| College degree or equivalent | .1 | .2 | .2 | .2 | .4 | 1.0 | 1.2 |
| Total | 123.7 | 173.7 | 164.5 | 184.9 | 232.6 | 274.0 | 229.0 |

SOURCE: *Statisticki Godisnjak*, 1964, p. 114.

eighteenth and nineteenth centuries. The unskilled workers in Western Europe flooded the market, and depressed the level of wages so that the owners of capital were able to accumulate large profits. The price paid by the workers for this enlarged accumulation of capital was a dear one; to quote Pope John's *Mater et Magistra*:

"While enormous riches accumulated in the hands of a few, the working classes found themselves in conditions of increasing hardship. Wages were insufficient or at starvation level, conditions of work were oppressive and without respect for physical health, moral behavior and religious faith.

"Especially inhuman were the working conditions to which children and women were subjected. The specter of unemployment was ever present and the family was exposed to a process of disintegration."

It is obvious that socialist countries in the process of their economic development had a great advantage. They found a ready-made technology which they could and did borrow. And also their governments have much greater power than West European governments had in early capitalism. However, the applicability of existing technological knowledge is not, at least not in the short run, automatic. First, there is the human factor, which sets limits to the amount of technology which can be borrowed. This bottleneck explains the emphasis on education in every socialist country. Second, to apply even a ready-made technology takes time. Buildings have to be built, machines to be made, and so on. This all calls for a diversion of resources from consumption to the lengthening of the roundabout process of production.

In Yugoslavia, however, the increased supply of workers cannot, as in nineteenth-century Western Europe, depress the wage rates, because wages are proposed by the Workers' Councils and approved by the local governments. The Yugoslav government could, of course, depress wages by its own unilateral action, but it would not be politically advisable. Also, enterprises are reluctant to hire new workers because of difficulties in laying them off, the result being an increase in the rate of unemployment in Yugoslavia. The high rate of investment activity and public works financed through the budget appear inadequate to create a sufficient number of new jobs for ever-increasing numbers of workers.

A number of writers have placed emphasis on education as one of the preconditions for successful economic development, for example, Schultz[23] and Zebot.[24] Their point is well taken but is not broad and explicit enough. Karl Marx made a real contribution when more than one hundred years ago, at a time when classical economists were engaged in predicting stagnation, he said that the world economy would develop enormously and in analyzing the conditions necessary to assure this development included working habits in the concept of productive forces.* This is an extremely important concept, the relevance of which has not been sufficiently emphasized by writers on the problems of economic development in the underdeveloped regions of Europe and in Africa, Asia, and South America.

In Yugoslavia, except in Slovenia and the northern parts of Serbia and Croatia, working habits are far from being developed. And this is as true for white-collar employees as for unskilled laborers. Thus a university student in Yugoslavia, though he may be getting the good education that Schultz and Zebot consider necessary, is not getting something else that is necessary. He has strong primary-group relations of the kind that are characteristic of pre-industrial societies: strong family ties that assure him of parental support, strong ties of comradeship with his fellow students that limit his competitiveness with them. Some factors that students in other cultures, with a different orientation, can handle readily simply reinforce the Yugoslav student's attitude – free tuition, stipends and fellowships, optional lectures, long summers on holiday. When he graduates, he may be good in his field but he lacks something more important: willingness to concentrate on his work and to wrestle with the problems he faces with a high degree of stubbornness and patience. He lacks application or, as the German term puts it, *Sitzfleisch*. This lack of those well-developed working habits which in the minds of Weber and Tawney are essential for the development of the capitalist economy explains why the growing labor force in Yugoslavia does not contribute to the rate of economic growth as much as it could, given the level of technology.[25]

If we specify that the development of working habits is part of true education, then we can agree with Schultz and Zebot. I do not mention this lack of working mentality in a derogatory sense. Working habits cannot be acquired overnight. However, the fact is that, except in Slovenia and parts of Serbia and Croatia, the working mentality in Yugoslavia today is not equal to that in the West. This difference in working habits within the country itself is visible from the remark made to me by a Yugoslav

*Marx was certainly not the first to understand the importance of education and working habits for the process of economic development. His contribution lies in the fact that he gave to these two concepts such a prominent place in his analysis of economic development.

economist. He said that it has been observed that the marginal productivity of capital is higher in Slovenia than in Macedonia. The investment funds spent in Slovenia result, on the average, in more efficient plants and a better quality of products.

Table 11 illustrates the differences in degree of economic development among the different Republics in Yugoslavia; these differences appear very significant.

Table 11. Value of Social Product in Dinars by People's Republics of Yugoslavia for 1959 (1959 Prices)

| Republic | Total [a] | Per Capita |
|---|---|---|
| Serbia | 934,427 | 124,308 |
| Croatia | 649,427 | 155,730 |
| Slovenia | 384,928 | 244,088 |
| Bosnia and Herzegovina | 329,338 | 99,738 |
| Macedonia | 112,301 | 81,792 |
| Montenegro | 35,395 | 72,382 |
| Total | 2,446,253 | 132,796 |

SOURCE: *Statisticki Godisnjak*, 1961, p. 350.
[a] In millions of dinars.

Table 12 illustrates the differences in the level of education in different parts of the country. These differences can be attributed to historical factors. For centuries Slovenia, Croatia, and parts of Serbia were ruled by Austria, a highly cultured and civilized nation. Serbia, Macedonia, Bosnia, and Herzegovina were ruled by the backward Turks. Montenegro preserved its independence, but centuries of uninterrupted war against the Turks absorbed all the energy and resources of the country.

The immobility of labor is another problem in Yugoslavia, one which can only have a restraining influence on the rate of economic growth. This

Table 12. Percentage of Population above Ten Years of Age with a Given Education in Five People's Republics

| Republic | No School | Grammar School | Technical School | Gymnasium | Higher Education | Not Known |
|---|---|---|---|---|---|---|
| Serbia | 45.6% | 42.8% | 7.8% | 2.8% | 0.6% | 0.4% |
| Croatia | 34.2 | 52.6 | 9.1 | 2.8 | 0.7 | 0.5 |
| Slovenia | 14.8 | 67.9 | 12.4 | 3.8 | 0.9 | 0.2 |
| Macedonia | 41.2 | 48.0 | 6.9 | 2.3 | 0.4 | 1.3 |
| Montenegro | 43.8 | 40.9 | 9.7 | 4.3 | 0.8 | 0.5 |

SOURCE: Derived from *Statisticki Godisnjak*, 1961, p. 67.

immobility of labor has two sources. Immobility among unskilled workers is due mostly to the fact that Yugoslavia is a multinational state with strong national sentiments which often amount to chauvinism. Because of this, surplus labor from one part of the country will not move to another part of the country. Among skilled blue-collar workers and university graduates immobility of labor caused by national feelings partly disappears. There are quite a few Slovenian and Croatian technicians today in Montenegro, especially in the city of Niksich, where one of the largest iron works in Yugoslavia is located, and there are also quite a few Serbs and Montenegrins in Croatia and Slovenia. Immobility of skilled workers and employees stems from a different origin. They are not willing to leave big cities or rich districts. In the late 1950's a young lawyer who would join the Federal or Republic administration and stay in Belgrade, Zagreb, Ljubljana, Sarajevo, Skoplje, or Titograd would have a starting salary of 17,500 dinars, whereas, if he was willing to go to work either for a local government or for an enterprise located in a small town, he could earn up to 40,000 dinars. Despite this, young people preferred to stay in the big cities. In a number of cases young university graduates in Belgrade accepted clerical work or even work in restaurants rather than leave the metropolis. The leading (and official Communist) Yugoslav daily paper *Borba* complained that out of 5,109 state farms and peasants' cooperatives only 139 had a specialist in agriculture, while at the same time in Vinkovci, a small but very rich town in Croatia, twenty agricultural specialists with university degrees were idling and living off their unemployment insurance.[26]

Statistical data on the productivity of labor in Yugoslavia are calculated on the basis of output per man-hour. This leaves out the contribution of capital. The shortcomings of a method of calculation which leaves out another factor of production, capital, are visible from the data in Table 13, from which it appears that the rate of productivity increase was higher in Montenegro than in any other Republic. This is of course an illusion; the introduction of only a few modern factories with up-to-date technology was sufficient to make for this fast rate of labor productivity increase. If the rate of productivity increase were calculated in accordance with Professor Kendrick's concept[27] of a combined labor-capital input the overall rate of productivity increase would be considerably smaller and Montenegro would probably be behind other, more developed Republics.

The Yugoslav government has paid a good deal of attention to the problem of the productivity of labor. As early as December 15, 1948, the Law on Inventions and Technical Improvements was enacted, providing material incentives to innovators and inventors. The Institute of Productivity of Labor was created in 1961 as a self-financing institution whose job is to discover and sell organizational and technical inventions to all who are interested in gaining from the increased productivity of labor. We have seen that in the Law on Investment Loans of July 25, 1956, the banks were instructed to consider research projects in contests for loans

Table 13. Chain Index of Labor Productivity in Industry

| Republic | 1957 | 1958 | 1959 | 1960 | 1961 | 1962 |
|---|---|---|---|---|---|---|
| Yugoslavia | 8.7 | 1.1 | 5.3 | 6.4 | 3.4 | 4.6 |
| Serbia | 9.5 | 3.6 | 4.1 | 5.5 | 3.2 | 5.6 |
| Croatia | 11.8 | −1.2 | 7.7 | 7.0 | 2.4 | 6.4 |
| Slovenia | 7.1 | −0.5 | 6.6 | 7.9 | 3.5 | 3.7 |
| Bosnia and Herzegovina | 5.5 | 3.5 | 5.0 | 3.8 | 3.2 | .9 |
| Macedonia | 5.0 | −0.3 | 0.6 | 7.3 | 8.7 | 3.0 |
| Montenegro | −9.4 | 7.8 | 11.8 | 25.1 | 11.5 | 3.7 |

SOURCE: *Statistical Pocketbook of Yugoslavia,* 1962, p. 54; 1962 data from *ibid.,* 1963, p. 55.

whenever such projects would seem to the bank to be of far-reaching scientific importance. In the period 1956–60 the value of grants for research projects increased from 57,000,000 dinars in 1956 to 8,865,000,-000 dinars in 1960.[28]

The performance of the Yugoslav economy has been rather satisfactory since 1953, i.e., since the implementation of the innovation of 1950–51. It is not the quantitative performance only but even more the qualitative composition of output, which has allowed the Yugoslavs to have a variety of domestically produced consumer goods, such as refrigerators, stoves, television sets, and automobiles. The fact that these products are available only to those in high income brackets, such as high party members, lawyers, doctors, university professors, and especially soccer players and engineers, does not detract from the fact that Yugoslav industry is producing these goods.

The factors which, given the huge amount of American aid, contributed most to economic development after 1953 might be arranged in the following order of importance: the changing pattern of investment springing from the emphasis on innovating actions in the organizational structure as well as in technical aspects of production, the high rate of accumulation of capital, and finally, the rapid increase in the number of people employed.

The darkest spot on the economy has been agriculture. Though people in East Europe are not underfed—Polish farmers are eating at least as well as before the war, and in Yugoslavia food is plentiful, thanks to a great extent to American aid—agriculture has failed to increase food surpluses in the quantities needed to assure proportional development of both industry and agriculture at the pace desired by the government. Besides political reasons for farmers' reluctance to work harder and better, there are also purely economic reasons, such as very high taxes, which may explain the lagging agricultural production in socialist countries. High tax rates tend to increase the relative value of leisure and diminish incentives to work. A high and progressive tax tends to make farmers work only as much as they need in order to feed their households, pay taxes, and buy the merest necessities. Table 14 shows how taxes on farmers in Yugoslavia take the majority of that income which remains after their personal consumption is deducted from their gross income.

Table 14. Income and Taxation in Agriculture by Private Sector in 1958

| Item | Billions of Dinars |
|---|---|
| *Income* | |
| Farmers' gross income | 455 |
| Farmers' private consumption | 394 |
| Savings[a] | 61 |
| *Taxation* | |
| Income tax | 32.9 |
| Communal tax | 17.4 |
| Total | 50.3 |
| Net savings[b] | 10.7 |

SOURCE: Adapted from Hoffman and Neal, *Yugoslavia and the New Communism,* p. 290.
[a] Gross income less farmers' consumption.
[b] Surplus over domestic consumptions.

A look at this combination of factors—the rate of growth in Yugoslavia since 1945, the pattern of investment, changes in the marginal capital-output ratio, and organizational changes in the Yugoslav economy – suggests that changes in the organizational framework in 1953 and 1954 pulled the country out of stagnation and that this new organizational framework influenced the pattern of investment by way of profit incentives. Once this new system was fully implemented, the Yugoslav economy grew, in the period 1956–60, at a very high and satisfactory rate. Assessing the state of the Yugoslav economy in 1960, the London *Economist* said, under the title "A Buoyant Economy":

Yugoslavia's economy is expanding so rapidly that the authorities have had to limit further short-term credits . . . industrial concerns have helped to increase imbalance in the economy by drawing too heavily on bank credit, for though they had themselves accumulated very large funds, these are being used not merely to finance investment but also to raise wages.[29]

and the New York *Times* said editorially:

More detached observers may understand that in such difficult unprecedented experimentation some mistakes are natural and lessons must be learned. . . . The Yugoslavs' troubles pale into insignificance by comparison with the distress and hunger produced by the kind of economic planning practiced in Russia under Stalin and today in China.[30]

Let us conclude the analysis of the macroeconomic aspect of the Yugoslav economy by setting the ground for the analytical explanation of the performance of the Yugoslav economy.

1. There has been a definite relationship between structural changes in the economy and the rate of growth. This does not, of course, prove causal relationship. The period of time under consideration permits us only to state our conclusion as a workable hypothesis, which should be tested in the years to come. Structural changes always influenced the change in the rate of growth in one or another direction, and the latter always responded to and never preceded the former. The first innovation, in 1946, turned out to be a failure. The rate of growth declined in the late 1940's and early 1950's. The second innovation began to be introduced *de facto* when the rate of growth was at its lowest. This innovation, unlike the first one, was quite successful and the rate of economic growth in Yugoslavia in the second part of the 1950's was quite high. And then after seven years the rate started to decline once more. Then the third innovation was introduced and the rate of growth rose from 4 per cent in 1962 to 12 per cent in 1963 and 10 per cent in 1964.

2. The analysis of the rate and pattern of investment in Yugoslavia shows that it was not the quantity of investment but its changing quality which pulled the economy out from stagnation.

3. The analysis of the Yugoslav economy since the last war shows that the first major innovation was followed by the imposition of a strict financial plan which relegated the banking system to an inferior role. The outcome of the first major innovation was that the rate of growth declined. The second major innovating action made the banking system relatively independent and abolished a strict financial plan. The result was a high rate of growth plus huge chronic deficits in the balance of payments.* The third major innovation continued to increase the independence and importance of the banking system.

*After his return from Yugoslavia in 1959, Galbraith reported in his book *Journey to Poland and Yugoslavia* that at the time of his visit the Yugoslav economists were engaged in a lively discussion regarding the negative balance of payments. One group favored an increase in foreign debt in order to secure an accelerated rate of growth. Another group called for more restraint in borrowing from foreign countries. See Appendix IV on foreign trade.

## IV THE FIRM IN YUGOSLAVIA

IN ORDER to ascertain the ability of the Yugoslav firm to innovate, i.e., to undertake actions not previously planned, and evaluate the strength of the system of incentives given to the potential innovator, we shall analyze the organization of the Yugoslav firm and its relations with the local government and the banking system.

### THE FOREIGN RELATIONS OF THE YUGOSLAV FIRM

By foreign relations of the enterprise we shall mean its relations with local government, which is the enterprise's direct political superior, and with the banking system, upon which the economic performance of the enterprise depends.

This chapter will not deal with the organization of the local government. Whatever its organization, it is an organ of the state and as such is a combination of a number of political, economic, and social functions pertaining to the area under its jurisdiction. We are interested only in its authority over the enterprise.

The Federal Government in Yugoslavia has no direct control over enterprises. The People's Republics have more control than the Federal Government because of their direct supervision of the local governments. There are no concealed remnants of direct political and administrative control over individual enterprises within the Federal Government. It exercises its political control indirectly through party channels and through the governments of the People's Republics,* and directly through the banks, which distribute funds from the G.I.F. according to the Social Plan.

*It is of course easy to imagine that the intentions of the Federal Government are reshaped, sometimes substantially, on their way through channels.

The entry of a new firm into an industry occurs on the initiative of the local government, social organizations, commercial organizations, or groups of citizens. The conditions to be met by the initiator are precisely prescribed and, when the initiator is the local government or a social or commercial organization, approval by the local government is a formality provided the legal conditions for the formation of a new enterprise have been met. However, the local government has a discretionary right to approve or reject an application for the formation of a new enterprise when it is submitted by a group of citizens, even if all legal conditions have been met. This discretionary right of the government sets a restraint on the freedom to innovate by means of new entry. There is an offsetting factor which should make the local government vitally interested in the opening of new profitable enterprises: the revenue of the local government depends in large part on the profits of the firms located in the territory under its jurisdiction (see Ch. I, pp. 32–34). If profits are high the revenue of the local government will be high. Although this factor contributes to the local government's willingness to approve new entries it still does not lift the bureaucratic controls; the local government will have to agree with the group of citizens concerning the future rentability of a new enterprise. It is by no means certain that the local government and the group of citizens will have the same anticipations about the success of the new enterprise. This is, of course, an important limitation on freedom to innovate.

The formation of a new enterprise imposes the problem of the supply of capital. In a free market economy capital is usually provided by the sale of shares which give their owners the right to participate in the affairs of the new enterprise. In Yugoslavia this way of financing new enterprises cannot be used because of the dogma that no one shall derive income from owning productive goods. The initiator of a new enterprise has to provide starting capital, which can be either money obtained from the bank (most often) or physical goods (when the local government transfers the capital assets of a liquidating enterprise to the new enterprise). The enterprise is under an obligation to use its capital with all possible care and eventually to increase it. The enterprise has no property rights over its capital, whether it be fixed or circulating; it has only the right of use (see Ch. I, p. 29). The local government has the right and duty to see that this right of use is not abused either by applying the capital to purposes other than the legal activity of the enterprise* or by a reckless

*This, of course, may be an additional limitation on the freedom to innovate.

attitude toward it by the employees. Any damage done to the capital assets must be repaired at the expense of the enterprise.

So far we have seen that the local government has a direct influence in forming new enterprises, in controlling the proper maintenance of capital assets by all the enterprises in its territory, and in controlling the legality of their economic activities. None of these limitations significantly affects the freedom to innovate of existing enterprises within the sphere of their regular activities. In addition to these three controls there are two more which will be analyzed later in this chapter. They deal with the participation of the local government in appointing the director of the enterprise and the influence exercised by the local government over the distribution of net profit.

The prerogatives of the local government place some controls on the freedom of the firm to innovate and on the freedom of new entry. It is the banking system that controls the availability of funds which the firm may need to carry out its actions.

These financial means can be allocated to the enterprise from the G.I.F. in the form of a bank loan. The enterprise has to compete for the money from the G.I.F. A denial of the loan to the enterprise by the bank could mean the end of its expansion. The Social Plan does not provide financial means of expansion directly to individual enterprises. The plan merely assures the enterprises that they will be able to carry on the process of simple reproduction; i.e., the enterprises will be able to use their amortization funds for maintaining production and capacity at a constant level. But to grow, the enterprise has to show vigor and ability to engage in an innovating activity which the bank will adjudge as sufficiently profitable. Since the outcome of the application for a bank loan depends to a large extent upon the submitted project and its approval by the bank, each enterprise is forced to pay a great deal of attention to its presentation. The explanation of the project should consist of three parts: the construction part (showing what would have to be built); the technical part (showing machines which would have to be bought, pointing out which of them can be bought within the country and which can be provided only from abroad, and a diagram showing the technological process of production); and the economic part. The latter part should show the following data: potential demand, availability of raw materials, conditions of transportation from the sources of raw material and to the market, availability of labor and especially of skilled labor, the exact location of the enterprise, amount of fixed and circulating capital needed, cost of production, profitability of the project, terms of repayment of the loan, and other facts.

To prepare such an elaborate project the enterprise must, as a rule, hire outside technical experts and economists. This multiplies expenses because the preparation of such projects is very costly, often as much as 1,000,000 dinars,[1] and still the enterprise cannot be sure of the outcome of its application. This introduces an additional element of uncertainty into the microeconomic aspect of the Yugoslav economy. The enterprise must seek the most profitable project because only then can it hope to influence, but not to decide or determine, the outcome of its investment plans. Investment funds become available subject to proof that the firm's project will satisfy more wants, backed by enough income to make their satisfaction profitable, than any other project competing for the same funds. Such complicated and costly applications for loans may have the effect that many potentially successful innovations are not undertaken.

In addition to money from the G.I.F., the enterprise can also apply for bank credit, in the same way in which an American enterprise would apply to any commercial bank. The Yugoslav enterprise may apply for credit to its communal bank and to any of the three specialized banks, depending, of course, on the nature of the investment. The banks may extend credit for the provision of fixed capital assets, for circulating capital assets of two kinds, permanent and supplementary, and for consumers' credit.[2]

The banks can give credit from their own free reserves. These free reserves are deposits, time deposits, money which the bank itself receives as credit (thus, specialized banks may get credit from the National Bank), and bank bonds.* From time deposits and from money collected by issuing bonds the banks can extend consumers' credit and credit for buying fixed capital assets and circulating capital assets. From deposits which may be withdrawn on request the banks can give only short-term credits, to be repaid within one year. This supplementary circulating capital differs from the permanent circulating capital in that it satisfies a short-run need to increase production or inventories because of holidays, good seasons, etc. Credits are, in general, allocated by means of a contest which the bank has to announce in the *Official Bulletin*. However, in the case of the specialized banks, the government may permit a direct contact between

*These are interest-bearing securities issued by the banks and redeemable at or before their maturity. They can be bought by individuals, enterprises, and cooperatives.

the bank and the applicant. There is in general no difference in the process of credit allocation and the allocation of money from the G.I.F. The banks are expected to follow the basic propositions of the Social Plan when allocating credits. The banks, however, have more freedom in moving credits from one use to another whenever the demand for funds justifies such transfer. This cannot be done with the money from the G.I.F. except by permission of the Federal Government.

The relationship between the firm and the banking system is crucial for the proper understanding of the Yugoslav economic system. The enterprise, despite internal financing, depends heavily on the banks. This dependence, however, is economic rather than political.* The banking system, in turn, is entrusted with the enormous responsibility of allocating investment funds among different alternatives within each industry. Both the fulfillment of the Social Plan and the maximization of consumers' utilities within the framework of the Social Plan depend on the efficiency of the banking system in discharging its duties. But there is a limit to what the banks can be expected to do with respect to the task of efficient resource allocation, at least as long as only 2.3 per cent of all employees in the Yugoslav banks have a B.A. degree or better.[3]

## THE INTERNAL ORGANIZATION OF THE YUGOSLAV FIRM

All the internal affairs of the Yugoslav firm can be logically divided into the right to manage and the right to operate the firm. The right to manage includes price-output decisions, wage determination, production planning, internal organization of the firm, disposition of the total revenue, final decisions concerning employment, firing and laying off, and approval of income statements. The right to operate the firm includes implementation of the decisions of those who manage the enterprise, control and organization of the process of production, responsibility for the best utilization of factors of production, and responsibility and control over the quality of product.

Since 1950–51, the right of management in Yugoslavia, within the limits determined by law, supposedly has been in the hands of the employees of each enterprise. Annually they elect their organ of management, the Workers' Council, which consists of 15 to 120 members, depending on the size of the enterprise. Council members are elected by

*Political considerations must not be neglected in Yugoslavia. However, the relationship between the firm and the bank seems to be primarily market-oriented.

secret ballot from among the employees. No outsider can be nominated and elected and no elected member receives extra payment for being on the Council. Furthermore, all members of the Workers' Council, including the chairman who is nominated by the members and from among the members, continue to work at their regular jobs; they do not get offices or any special benefits. They are reimbursed only for lost earnings while participating in the discharge of their duties. To assure that unskilled as well as skilled workers are represented on the Council, the law provides that 75 per cent of the members of the Workers' Council must be blue-collar workers. The government also wants to see an increased turnover among the workers who are on the Council and provides that each year only one-half of the Council can be re-elected, so that new workers always come onto the Council but at the same time continuity is assured.

The question of the scope of independence of the Workers' Councils from their local governments is not too important. It is important that this institution exists; now that it is there it will slowly become entrenched in the workers' minds. Benjamin Ward, writing about Workers' Councils through 1955, said that their real rights were rather small, [4] but explaining the situation in 1957 he said that the enterprise was independent, and that though there was the possibility of government intervention, it could be regarded as an exception.[5] The enterprises have definite independence in deciding the quantity and quality of output. They have their say concerning the appointment of the director, wage determination, and distribution of profit. Regardless of the extent of interference in the work of the Workers' Councils by the local government, the mere fact that the workers have the right to make some decisions is significant.

From the static aspect the institution of the Workers' Council does not appear very promising and attractive. Management involves a skill and a talent different from the skills and talents of execution. Adam Smith said that division of functions is the secret of efficiency. The institution of the Workers' Council tends to re-delegate to the workers the rights and duties of managing the firm and, at the same time, it tends to make the managerial class a mere executor of the decisions made by the workers.

However, the role of the institution of the Workers' Council may be assessed from its dynamic as well as its static aspect. It appears in a completely different light when analyzed in historical perspective. *Given the present social system* in Yugoslavia, the role of the institution of the

Workers' Council has significance for the future from both the economic and sociopolitical aspect.

From the economic aspect the institution of the Workers' Council is reminiscent of the role played by stockholders in a free-market economy. Given the present functional relationship between profits and earnings the Workers' Council acts as a force pushing the director to seek ever higher profits. The workers, though they do not know much about the art of management, know surprisingly well how to compare their earnings with the earnings of other workers employed by enterprises engaged in similar economic activity. If they find their earnings lower than those of other workers, the director of the low-profit firm may find himself fired. The director is forced to use all his talents to secure at least an average rate of profit for the enterprise. Within the framework of the present social system in Yugoslavia it is better for both the employees and the economy as a whole that the economic performance of the enterprise is in the hands of the employees rather than the bureaucrats in the central government. By striving for higher wages the employees force the director to strive for ever larger profits. The director's search for profits calls for an increasing flow of innovations. The allocation of resources tends, under these circumstances, to conform to consumers' preferences, subject to the constraints of the distribution of income, the tax structure, and the basic propositions of the Social Plan. On this point one can agree with Dunlop,[6] who says that the full impact of the institution of the Workers' Council on economic development in Yugoslavia can be properly understood only when the role of the Workers' Council is observed in its dynamic context. For Dunlop, the relation between director and Workers' Council means that the former can be neither a dictator nor a paternalistic supervisor. He has to sell his ideas and to convince the Workers' Council that his ideas are sound. Consequently, there is every reason to believe that the director will try to make his proposals constructive, the result being an improvement in the allocation of resources with respect to consumers' preferences.

From the sociopolitical aspect, the Workers' Council seems to be the only important institution within the framework of the Yugoslav socioeconomic system which is not necessarily controlled by the Party from inside—because of the system of rotation. As long as wages are a function of the size of the profit of the enterprise, the Workers' Council, fighting for better wages via higher profits, will act as the force moving the economic system toward more freedom for the enterprise from the government. The firm acceptance of this institution by the workers and its dynamic potentialities may eventually force the bureaucracy to choose between further decentralization of the economic system and a retreat to the old system of administrative control. But "as time goes by, it may become increasingly difficult for those who . . . favor . . . bureaucratic control . . . to effectuate the return to rigid centralism."[7] If the government finds it impossible ever to effectuate this return to rigid centralism the institution of the Workers' Council should be given full credit. After a temporary decline in the rate of economic growth in 1961 and 1962, some Yugoslav officials used the opportunity to try to reverse the trend of organizational changes back toward the rigid centralized system. It seemed that Tito sided with them, to judge from his strong speech in Split on May 25, 1962. However, only a few months later Tito stated that "some key officials did not have enough faith in the Workers' Councils. We changed them."[8] He also declared that his criticism of the state of the national economy expressed in the May speech was perverted by some, and called a halt to further attacks on the managers' freedom of initiative.[9]

Since the Workers' Council is rather a huge body, it selects from its members an Executive Board, which consists of three to eleven members plus the director of the enterprise. The members of the Executive Board (except the director) are elected every year, and no one can be a member for more than two terms. The duties of the Executive Council can be divided into three broad groups: to prepare proposals for the Workers' Council, to control the execution of Council decisions, and to perform some independent functions, such as promotions, training of workers, and monthly operating plans.

Until 1953 the director of an enterprise was a representative of the state, and his position with respect to the employees was much stronger than it is now, when he is elected by a commission appointed by the local government and the Workers' Council. Furthermore, the Workers' Council can propose to the local government that the director be fired.* True,

* "In 1956, for instance, out of a total of 6,079 directors of enterprises, . . . 502 were dismissed. Causes for dismissal included laxity in the case of 82 dismissals, economic crimes in the case of 59 and 'other reasons' for 422. The workers' bodies initiated 168 firings, governmental bodies (in most cases local governments) 314 and the Party 20" (Hoffman and Neal, *Yugoslavia and the New Communism*, p. 242).

the local government may reject the proposal of the Workers' Council, but this right of the Council gives the local government an opportunity to supervise the actions of the director. And since the director never knows how successful the proposal for his firing may be, he must consider the requests made by the Workers' Council. The director is responsible for the implementation of the decisions of the Workers' Council, for efficient production of the enterprise, for submitting proposals dealing with financial and production questions to the Workers' Council, and similar tasks. The director, in his job, is helped by the commercial, technical, and other departments.

It appears that the operation of the Yugoslav enterprise is under the direct influence of the Workers' Council, the local government, and the director. If the president of the local government is a local man, the chances are that he will be interested in the promotion of any profitable enterprise in its territory. Even more than that, the president can influence the commission to select a director who has the ability to promote the enterprise and thereby increase the revenue of the local government.* Even when there is a disagreement among the effective leaders of the three institutions, if one of them is determined and able to carry out his ideas he may be successful in the end. There is almost a textbook example from Cetinje. Immediately after 1951 the director of a small shop, *Obod*, in Cetinje sensed the full impact of the forthcoming changes and, in spite of local opposition, took the initiative in making *Obod* a large enterprise. In 1954, this enterprise was among the first in Yugoslavia to start producing refrigerators and electric stoves of good quality, and now is producing 2,000 units monthly.[10] At the same time any of these effective leaders, and this is especially true of the director because of his position as the operational leader, may render the system vulnerable to economic crimes.† Examples are ample and can be found in the Yugoslav press. For example, *Borba*, the official paper of the Party, reported on February

*In a number of cases, once the economy was put on a profit and loss basis and the local government's revenues were made dependent upon the profit of the enterprises, the local governments took a new attitude toward the people known to be successful businessmen. It is common knowledge in Yugoslavia that a number of prewar businessmen were offered jobs either by local governments or by the enterprises.

†One should not jump to the conclusion that the Yugoslav economy is more vulnerable to different kinds of malversations than that of the United States or U.S.S.R. The problem we are exploring here is who in Yugoslavia can perform economic crimes, and in what ways. Economic crimes are being performed daily in every country.

3, 1962, that the director of the enterprise *Galeb* in Ohrid, Macedonia, took 1,262,000 dinars from the enterprise for his official trips during 1961, and was able, when caught, to account for only about 300,000 dinars. On March 15, 1962, *Borba* mentioned another case, this time in Maribor, Slovenia. The director of the enterprise *Surovina* falsified reports of expenditures for raw materials and other operating expenses and in a few months pocketed about 10,000,000 dinars. It can be asserted that within the broad framework of the Social Plan the performance and the success of the Yugoslav enterprise depends to a large extent upon the ability, willingness, and integrity of three key men: the director and the effective leaders of the local government and the Workers' Council. They can do much good within the organizational framework of the economy, or they can destroy the enterprise as well as themselves.

The main scheme of the distribution of the total revenue of the Yugoslav firm was discussed earlier and only a few comments need be added.*

The first item in the distribution of total revenue is the *expenditures on raw materials* and *other operating expenses*, which include the repayment of short-run credits obtained from the bank during the rush season or in cases of emergency when the enterprise needed extra money to increase its inventories or to step up production; insurance payments to the state insurance company (every enterprise is asked to insure its capital up to the amount of its value less accumulated depreciation); payments for services of persons who are not employed by the enterprise, e.g., hired experts who prepare investment projects for the enterprise; transportation expenses; official trips of the employees; 90 per cent of advertising expenses.†

The second item is the payment for *depreciated value* of the fixed capital assets. The value of an asset is determined on the basis of the price paid for it, cost of installation, transportation expenses, expected major repairs, minus its scrap value. For prewar assets, a special approach has been devised. They were first re-evaluated in 1952 and then a deduction from the value of the asset ranging from 5 to 40 per cent was

*The terms *revenue*, *income*, and *profit* are not a direct translation from Serbo-Croatian. They are used to make the scheme of the total revenue distribution comparable to the revenue distribution of a firm in the United States. The terms used in Yugoslavia and our translation are as follows: prihod — revenue; dohodak — income; dobit — profit.

† Ten per cent of the cost of advertising is not tax deductible.

permitted. Hence, the final formula for calculating depreciation on prewar assets is:

$$V_m = V \times \frac{100 - X}{100},$$

where $V_m$ = value of an asset on which amortization is to be paid, V = present value (re-evaluated value of prewar asset), and X = rate of obsolescence.

The rate of amortization is determined by dividing $V_m$ by the number of years the asset is expected to last.[11] The enterprise has the right to use its amortization funds for maintaining its assets and for purchasing new assets. In order to channel investments in the direction of its choice, however, the state kept some of these funds frozen. This was especially true of those assets that had to be bought abroad. The total yearly amount of amortization paid by all Yugoslav enterprises is around 200 billion dinars, about 30 billion dinars of which were blocked and channeled into different assets. The practice of amortization ceased in January 1961.[12]

The third item in the scheme of revenue distribution is the so-called *social contributions*, i.e., interest on the value of fixed capital assets adjusted for the amount depreciated, interest on the value of circulating capital, and rent. Interest is, in general, 6 per cent of the total value of capital. For some economic activities the government prescribes a lower rate of interest in order to promote them. This is the case in coal mining, where the rate of interest is fixed at 4 per cent, transportation and catering, where the rate of interest is 2 per cent, the electrical industry, with a rate of interest of 1.1 per cent, and cooperatives and state farms, which pay no interest on capital.[13] The inability of the firm to pay this interest after the payments for operating expenses and amortization leads to the compulsory liquidation of the enterprise. This is in fact the payment to the government for the right of use. The government uses this money, in general, for enlarging the Social Investment Fund, but can decide to transfer part of it to the budget for covering its administrative and other expenses. In any case, this is a federal receipt. What is the rationale of the payment? First, the government hopes that this payment will stabilize revenue going into investment funds and the budget; second, it is hoped that this payment will help improve economic efficiency. Since the payment is fixed regardless of the level of production and sales, it pays the enterprise operating for profit to maximize the utilization of its capital assets.*

Rent is the payment imposed upon the enterprises engaged in mining and operating under favorable natural conditions. Rent is independent of interest on capital. The process of determining rent is rather vague. It is said that precise regulations are being prepared. Rent is paid as a percentage of total proceeds. For example, the coal mining enterprise *Banovici*, in Bosnia, pays 4 per cent of its total sales as rent. The proceeds of this rent are divided as follows: 70 per cent to the Federal Budget, 15 per cent to the People's Republic, and 15 per cent to the local government in whose territory the enterprise is located.[14] Rent is intended to level off the advantages which one enterprise can have over another because of favorable natural conditions.

The fourth item is *turnover tax*. The significance of this tax lies in its reallocative function. This tax helps the government control the composition of output without having to fall back on the administrative-command system of planning.

The crucial variable upon which the success of this instrument of fiscal policy depends is the cross-elasticity of demand. The more correct the government estimate of the cross-elasticities of demand for different goods, the more successful the use of the turnover tax will be.

To analyze the effect of turnover tax, let us use the following symbols: $X =$ amount of commodity produced and sold per unit of time; $P_X (1 - t) =$ price received by the producer; $t =$ turnover tax rate; $P_X =$ price paid by the consumer; $X = aL^{1/2}, C^{1/2}$, the production function; $P_L = f(L)$, price of labor; and $P_C = f(C)$, price of capital. Taking $P_L$ and $P_X$ as parameters and assuming that $C \times P_C$ is fixed for each firm, the production function can be written as $X = a\sqrt{L}$.

The Yugoslav firm is a profit-oriented productive unit whose gross profit with respect to labor is at a maximum when

$$\frac{\Delta \Pi}{\Delta L} = \frac{a}{2\sqrt{L}} P_X (1 - t) - P_L = 0.$$

From this the firm can calculate its optimal demand for labor:

*Assume that fixed capital is one million dinars, and that circulating capital is a like amount. Now, regardless of the level of production and the amount of gross revenue, the enterprise pays 120,000 dinars to the Federal Government for the right of use. A profit-seeking enterprise has, of course, a good reason not to create overcapacity of its fixed capital and to use its circulating capital as efficiently as possible.

$$\frac{a}{2\sqrt{L}} = \frac{P_L}{P_X\,(1-t)},$$

where $a/(2\sqrt{L})$ equals marginal physical productivity of labor. Therefore,

$$2\sqrt{L} = \frac{aP_X\,(1-t)}{P_L},$$

$$4L = \left(\frac{aP_X\,(1-t)}{P_L}\right)^2, \text{ and } L = \tfrac{1}{4}\left(\frac{aP_X\,(1-t)}{P_L}\right)^2,$$

where L equals optimal demand for labor.

Given the production function, the lower the turnover tax rate, the greater the demand for labor and the larger the output.

Table 15. Tax on Profits of Enterprises

| Gross Profit[a] | Tax Rate |
|---|---|
| Before December 3, 1958 | |
| 0–25 | No tax |
| 25–40 | 0 + 25%[b] |
| 40–60 | 9.375% + 62% |
| 60–80 | 26.92% + 70% |
| 80 and up | 37.69% + 72% |
| After December 3, 1958 | |
| 0–20 | No tax |
| 20–40 | 0 + 25% |
| 40–55 | 12.5% + 50% |
| 55–70 | 22.73% + 60% |
| 70–85 | 30.73% + 65% |
| 85–100 | 36.77% + 68% |
| 100 and up | 41.45% + 70% |

SOURCE: *Sluzbeni List*, December 18, 1957, Pravni Akt 648, and December 3, 1958, Pravni Akt 811.

[a] As percentage of the wage bill.

[b] This reads: "zero tax on 25 per cent and 25 per cent tax on the amount of profit in excess of 25 per cent of the wage bill."

The remainder is the *gross profit* of the enterprise. A federal tax of 15 per cent is paid out of the firm's gross profit. Before 1961, the firm paid a progressive tax according to the two scales shown in Table 15. On December 3, 1958, the scale was changed to the one shown in the bottom half of Table 15. To illustrate the meaning of the changing scale, let us assume that the payroll is 1,000 dinars and that gross profits are those shown in Table 16. Clearly, the modifications of 1958 aimed at making profits more attractive. If we now include in our comparison the flat 15 per cent tax of 1961 on the combined profits and wage bill, we find the amounts going to the federal treasury set down in Table 17.

Table 16. Comparative Tax on Profit in 1957 and 1958

| Enterprise | Profits[a] | Wage Bill[a] | Profits/ Wage Bill | Tax in 1957[a] | Tax in 1958[a] |
|---|---|---|---|---|---|
| A | 300 | 1,000 | 30 | 12.50 | 12.50 |
| B | 500 | 1,000 | 50 | 99.53 | 100.00 |
| C | 700 | 1,000 | 70 | 231.52 | 215.11 |
| D | 1,100 | 1,000 | 110 | 517.52 | 484.50 |

[a] In dinars.

Table 17. Comparative Tax on Profits in 1957, 1958, and 1961 (in Dinars)

| Enterprise | 1957 Scale | 1958 Scale | 1961 Scale |
|---|---|---|---|
| A | 12.5 | 12.5 | 195 |
| B | 99.53 | 100.0 | 225 |
| C | 231.52 | 215.11 | 255 |
| D | 517.52 | 484.50 | 315 |

The reform of 1961 made high profits even more attractive, but it imposed at the same time a heavy burden upon low-profit firms.

The reform of 1961 tends to increase the federal revenue. There is no reason to believe that the majority of firms in Yugoslavia are highly profitable, and, as Enterprises A and B show, the firms with low and moderate profits had their taxes increased the most. Furthermore, the scheme of 1961 included the total wage bill in the accounting concept of gross profit of the firm, enlarging the taxable income (relative to the 1957 scheme) by the amount of the total wage bill minus additional payments to the employees of the firm. Prior to 1961, the basic wage fund had to be deducted from the revenue of the firm before the profit tax was calculated.

The full effect of this flat tax rate depends on the way in which the government decides to use its additional revenue. If it goes into the budget the effect may be an increase in the satisfaction of government preferences. If this extra revenue goes into the G.I.F. the result may easily be further reconciliation between consumers' and planners' preferences—

assuming, of course, that funds from the G.I.F. will continue to be distributed in accordance with the ratio of value added to the amount of investment.

The net profit of the firm is distributed between the wage fund and the internal funds by applying the guideline described in Chapter III (pp. 73–75).

The problem of the determination of wage rates is in the hands of the Workers' Councils. The Workers' Council of the firm classifies jobs in accordance with the type of the work rather than on the basis of individual or collective bargaining – except for highly skilled workers, who, being in short supply, can write their own ticket. This classification can be done in a number of ways, the most frequent one being the point system. The Councils give each job a number of points according to the skill required, the expected intensity of work, and the working conditions in that particular job. At the same time the Council determines classes and pay per point for each class. Finally, by simple application of the number of points for each working place to the class to which it belongs, the firm determines the participation of each worker in the distribution of the wage fund. Whatever the system of remuneration from the wage fund is, the law requires the Workers' Council to announce it publicly, and to have it approved by the local government.

Before 1961, the firm paid a progressive tax on the amount of its net profit distributed among the employees. The tax was 10–40 per cent of the amount received by the workers in excess of their basic pay. As of 1961, the tax is 15 per cent and is divided equally between the local government and the People's Republic, going into their respective budgets.

The internal funds of the firm are the reserve fund, the working capital fund, and the collective consumption fund. The Workers' Council is free to distribute resources among these three funds subject to the minimum reserve fund requirement.

The working capital fund serves to finance regular expenditures in connection with the process of production and also to help expansion of the firm via internal financing. The collective consumption fund serves to finance unproductive expenditures, such as erection of apartments for workers, stipends to promising students, and vacation subsidies. A tax of 20 per cent is levied against resources allocated to the working capital fund and the collective consumption fund. The tax is divided equally between the local government and the People's Republic, going into their respective investment funds.

Here lies a built-in incentive for the local government to allow and encourage an increase in the wage fund relative to the internal funds of the firm. The tax charged against the internal funds can be used for investment purposes only, while the wage fund tax belongs to the budget of the local government and can be used for a number of purposes including an increase in the local government payroll.

As illustrations of this analysis, three income statements are given in Tables 18, 19, and 20. Although the only available data are for the years 1958 and 1959, collected and published in 1960, their importance is not diminished by this fact. They illustrate the microeconomic effects of the second major innovation, that of 1950–51, and, except for the inclusion of the wage fund in the concept of profit and the change in the

Table 18. Income Statements of *Metalna* of Maribor, Slovenia [a]

| Item | 1958 | 1959 |
|---|---|---|
| Total revenue | 4,791.1 | 6,597.5 |
| Less: | | |
| Amortization | 156.2 | 179.7 |
| Material expenditures | 3,341.9 | 4,494.4 |
| Income of the enterprise | 1,293.0 | 1,923.4 |
| Less: | | |
| Turnover tax | 17.0 | 20.4 |
| Interest on fixed capital (6%) | 145.0 | 151.7 |
| Interest on circulating capital (6%) | 139.0 | 178.6 |
| Rent and other contributions | 31.8 | 43.0 |
| Social security and similar payments | 77.8 | 101.6 |
| Payroll | 433.4 | 603.8 |
| Gross profit | 449.0 | 824.3 |
| Less: | | |
| Federal tax | 163.6 | 260.4 |
| Local government and People's Republic taxes | 34.0 | 52.5 |
| Net profit | 251.4 | 511.4 |
| Less: | | |
| Additional income to the employees | 213.0 | 311.1 |
| Extra tax | 2.8 | 0 |
| Reserve Fund | 25.0 | 65.5 |
| Other funds | 10.6 | 134.8 |
| Number of workers | 1,498 | 2,142 |
| Capital-labor ratio [b] | 3,688,100 | 2,669,900 |

SOURCE: *Pregled Podataka iz Zavrsnih Racuna Rudarskih i Privrednih Organisacija za 1958 i 1959* (Belgrade: Narodna Banka Jugoslavije, 1960), pp. 100–101.

[a] All but the last two items are in millions of dinars.

[b] The ratio of the value of capital to the number of workers.

tax structure, all items retained their old meaning and significance in the 1961 scheme of revenue disposition.

These three income statements seem to confirm the heavy emphasis on profit incentives in the Yugoslav economy. From the three statements we can observe, in Table 21, the relation between profits of a firm and the earnings of its employees.

Table 19. Income Statements of *Tovarja Poljoprivrednih Sprava* of Kostajnica, Bosnia [a]

| Item | 1958 | 1959 |
|---|---|---|
| Total revenue | 80.8 | 151.3 |
| Less: | | |
| Amortization | 2.4 | 3.0 |
| Material expenditures | 55.5 | 101.4 |
| Income of the enterprise | 22.9 | 46.9 |
| Less: | | |
| Turnover tax | 0 | 0 |
| Interest on fixed capital (6%) | .9 | 1.8 |
| Interest on circulating capital (6%) | 1.8 | 3.1 |
| Rent and other contributions | .7 | 1.0 |
| Social security and similar payments | 2.5 | 3.2 |
| Payroll | 13.3 | 20.6 |
| Gross profit | 3.7 | 17.2 |
| Less: | | |
| Federal tax | 0 | 3.6 |
| Local government and People's Republic taxes | 0 | .2 |
| Net profit | 3.7 | 13.4 |
| Less: | | |
| Additional income to the employees | 3.7 | 8.9 |
| Extra tax | 0 | 0 |
| Reserve fund | 0 | 1.5 |
| Other funds | 0 | 3.0 |
| Number of workers | 71 | 120 |
| Capital-labor ratio [b] | 1,476,000 | 1,272,500 |

SOURCE: *Pregled Podataka iz Zavrsnih Racuna Rudarskih i Privrednih Organisacija za 1958 i 1959*, pp. 100–101.

[a] All but the last two items are in millions of dinars.

[b] The ratio of the value of capital to the number of workers.

The statements also show some of the discriminatory features of the Yugoslav policy of taxation. While *Metalna* paid a rather high tax to the federal treasury, *Vaga* paid no tax on profit. *Tovarja Poljoprivrednih Sprava*, on the other hand, did not pay the turnover tax. If we calculate for each firm the ratio of the total of all taxes to income for 1959, we get the following percentages: *Metalna* paid 37 per cent of its income as a tax; *Tovarja Poljoprivrednih Sprava,* 21 per cent; and *Vaga*, 45 per cent.

Table 20. Income Statements of *Vaga* of Zagreb, Croatia[a]

| Item | 1959 |
|---|---|
| Total revenue | 114.4 |
| Less: | |
| Amortization | 3.9 |
| Material expenditures | 63.2 |
| Income of the enterprise | 47.5 |
| Less: | |
| Turnover tax | 11.4 |
| Interest on fixed capital (6%) | 1.5 |
| Interest on circulating capital (6%) | 6.9 |
| Rent and other contributions | 1.4 |
| Social security and similar payments | 2.4 |
| Payroll | 29.7[b] |
| Gross profit | −5.8 |
| Less: | |
| Federal tax | 0 |
| Local government and People's Republic taxes | 0 |
| Net profit | 0 |
| Less: | |
| Additional income to the employees | 0 |
| Extra tax | 0 |
| Reserve fund | 0 |
| Other funds | 0 |
| Number of workers | 107 |
| Capital-labor ratio [c] | 768.2 |

SOURCE: *Pregled Podataka iz Zavrsnih Racuna Rudarskih i Privrednih Organisacija za 1958 i 1959*, pp. 144–145.

[a] All but the last two items are in millions of dinars.

[b] Paid out 23.9 million dinars.

[c] The ratio of the value of capital to the number of workers.

Table 21. Relation between Profits of a Firm and Earnings of Its Employees (in Thousands of Dinars)

| Average Annual Earning per Worker | Metalna | | Tovarja Poljoprivrednih Sprava | | Vaga |
|---|---|---|---|---|---|
| | 1958 | 1959 | 1958 | 1959 | 1959 |
| Basic wage | 288.3 | 281.9 | 187.3 | 177.7 | 277.6 |
| Additional pay from profit | 142.0 | 145.2 | 52.1 | 74.7 | −54.2 |
| Total | 430.3 | 427.1 | 239.4 | 252.4 | 233.4 |

## THE PRICE-OUTPUT POLICY OF THE YUGOSLAV FIRM

If the behavior of the Yugoslav firm is inspired by the aim of maximizing profits, the price policy of the government can have definite reallocative effects. Furthermore, the government can rely on purely economic measures, such as fiscal and monetary policies, including price regulations, to control the level and composition of output.

The fact that prices of most goods and services in Yugoslavia are controlled suggests that there exists a set of government objectives different from true consumers' preferences, objectives which the controlled prices are supposed to realize. To achieve its objectives the government must modify market prices, but it must not ignore them. In other words, prices must be regulated in such a way as to bring together government objectives and the output decision of the profit-maximizing firm. It could be argued that the degree to which market prices are modified can serve as a useful yardstick for measuring the differences between the government scale of preference and true consumers' preferences.

The Yugoslav economists have worked out several price categories, each of which may be taken as representing a definite market structure.[15]

1. *Market prices*. There are no statistics available to indicate the size of this sector of the economy. It must be quite large, however, because most agricultural products are not price-regulated. The firms operating in this sector of the economy maximize their profits in about the same manner as any firm in the West. In this sector of the economy there seems to be a complete coincidence between true consumers' preferences and government objectives.

2. *Modified market prices*. Some prices are not directly regulated but are influenced by economic instruments such as the turnover tax, payments for the right of use, and availability of credits. These discriminatory modifications were observed in the income statements above. This price category includes a number of goods produced in manufacturing industries. Given the prevailing income distribution and the structure of consumers' wants, the firm operating in this market finds its best price-output level at a point different from its potential market solution. Through the system of preferential taxes and other economic instruments the government changes the position and slope of the firm's cost curves, thus changing its potential market-determined output decision, which in turn means a change in the amount of resources employed by the firm, and ultimately by the industry.

3. *Prices with an upper ceiling.* For some prices the price commission determines the upper limit, taking into account the prevailing production costs and applying to them the average rate of profit. For example, on May 23, 1962, the upper limit of the wholesale price of meat was set at cost plus 10 dinars per kilogram. The majority of prices in Yugoslavia belong to this category. Yugoslav economists believe that this price category serves two far-reaching goals: it safeguards consumers and it promotes cost-saving innovations. In case of an increase in costs which would threaten to squeeze the profit margin, the firm can petition the price commission to lift the price ceiling. On February 28, 1962, the *Tomos* factory in Slovenia asked the price commission to permit an increase in the price of their cars from 1,400,000 to 1,550,000 dinars.[16] If the price ceiling of a product is set above its profit-maximizing price the price-output decision of the firm will be similar to the one arrived at in the free market and there is no reallocative effect. If the price ceiling is set below the product's profit-maximizing price the firm will be earning less than its potential maximum profits and will find it necessary to use more resources than otherwise. It seems that this particular price category can be used to foster production but not to discourage it – unless, of course, the firms in the industry operate under different cost conditions. Then, if the price ceiling is set below the average cost curves of a number of relatively inefficient firms, these firms will be driven out of production and the rise of oligopoly will follow.

# V ANALYTICAL EXPLANATION OF THE PERFORMANCE OF THE YUGOSLAV ECONOMY

THE purpose of this chapter is to provide an analytical explanation of the process of organizational changes and the performance of the Yugoslav economy. It will be shown that the Schumpeter theory of economic development gives a meaningful analytical insight into the process and results of changes in the Yugoslav economy since 1945.

Although the problem of economic development has been in the focus of economic theory for some time, an agreed-upon definition of the concept of economic development is still lacking. Our working definition of the concept of economic development will be as follows: *Economic development consists of economic activities aiming at the satisfaction of both unsatisfied wants and potential wants, whether they be those of individuals, organized groups, or the government itself.*

In the following pages an attempt will be made to justify the reliance on the Schumpeter analysis of the process of economic development.* It is my contention that both the working definition of the concept of economic development and the results arrived at in Chapters I–IV are reasonably well explained by the theory of economic development of Joseph Schumpeter.

Let us start the analysis by outlining the evolution of the classical economic model, which was built on the assumptions of free competition, free entry, the labor theory of value, and rugged individualism. In this way the dynamic theory of Schumpeter will be placed in its proper historical perspective.

A number of factors, among which were the philosophical doctrines of

*This justification has to be a condensed and somewhat superficial one because the intent of this chapter is to relate Schumpeter's concept of economic development to the process of economic change in Yugoslavia and not to analyze the validity of his theory. For a brief review of his theory, see Appendix III.

nominalism and rationalism, new geographical and technological discoveries, and the Reformation,[1] destroyed the medieval patterns of life and established new ones. A new era of liberalism and individualism was born. The basic tendency of liberalism was "freedom from," from established political and social institutions, from the interference of the state in business activity, and from ecclesiastical regulations, courts, and ethics. This "freedom from" attitude rests on the conviction that there is a natural, rational, providential agreement that warrants this freedom and gives it primacy over any form of external authority. This freedom implies one's own responsibility for all activities in which he engages. Since society is, for traditional liberals, nothing but the sum total of individual buying and selling contracts, there is no room in the natural system of economic liberty for social ethics. If each individual follows his own self-interest, as he is expected to, competition is the necessary consequence. Once all individuals are engaged in competition among themselves the system will attain the equilibrium at which the satisfaction of individual wants will be maximized. In order to reach this equilibrium there should be no interference with the working of the market mechanism either by the state or by any other organized pressure group.

Marx was, except for the early socialists, the first elaborate and serious critic of the concept of unfettered market (or free) competition. Marx denied that free competition can maximize the happiness of all. He tried to show that it cannot because wants of equal urgency are not equally satisfied, their satisfaction being preconditioned by the ability (e.g., money incomes) to satisfy them. And his contention was that, because of an initial inequality which put some men at the disposal of others, economic and social inequality will tend to widen through the mechanism of free competition. At this point Marx divorced himself from the early socialists. He said that mankind must go through this increasing inequality if it wishes to attain any stage of affluence. The early socialists, on the other hand, seeing the "bad effects" of free competition, wanted to change the economic system.

With the beginning of the twentieth century and especially after the First World War, it became evident that the concept of free competition, as a theoretical model reflecting reality at least *in abstracto*, is more than doubtful. The ideal society as envisaged by the liberals of the nineteenth century was one in which all individuals are free and equal before the law. The liberals failed to recognize that equal rights do not mean an actual equality. The liberals wanted and preached a contractual society but failed to see that the parties to the contracts would not have the same bargaining power.* It was still a structured society in spite of personal freedom and equality before the law. "Ranks" and "orders" were destroyed, but a new phenomenon had appeared — a class society. This new division was based on the distribution of property.

In the nineteenth century, dependent workers constituted a majority in society and were victims of the industrial system. "They did not receive that to which they were . . . entitled: the rights of property were the wrongs of the poor. They could only secure their proper place in society by concerted action, what was called in the language of the day, union."[2] In the individualistic society as envisaged by classical economists, wage rates were supposed to be fixed exclusively through the market without the intervention of noneconomic pressures on either side. The workers, however, had weak bargaining power and could not obtain from their employers wages equal to the potential market price of labor. They organized into trade unions, i.e., organizations formed to remedy market injustices. Businessmen, in turn, expanded the scope of their associations.[3] This shift from individuals to groups was not in accordance with some predetermined plan but a spontaneous exercise of man's intellect and will in spite of and contrary to all dogmas of "the system of natural liberty." As Pope John XXIII wrote, "Socialization is not a product of natural forces working in a *deterministic* way. It is on the contrary . . . a creation of man . . . *free* . . . to work in a responsible way." In this passage from *Mater et Magistra* (italics mine) Pope John observes that the world moves not according to some predetermined model or plan but in accordance with the innovating actions of men, and these actions can be neither predicted nor ordered.

In view of the changing circumstances economic theory also had to change. New analytical instruments developed (e.g., marginal analysis), mirroring the real world more accurately than the classical analytical apparatus based on the labor theory of value. Two distinct schools developed from this point, one which stressed the importance of asking *why* and *how* economic changes take place and another which stressed the importance of analyzing the *consequences* of economic changes.

*The United States government enacted the Sherman Act in 1890, hoping that the implementation of this law would minimize the extent of the big monopoly powers.

Among the major exponents of the latter group are E. H. Chamberlin and Joan Robinson, who, in the field of analytical abstractions, postulated the necessary conditions which render market competition effective. For Chamberlin these postulates are: free entry, a large number of producers, and homogeneous products. Mrs. Robinson added to these two more postulates: perfect knowledge and perfect mobility of factors of production among different industries. Fellner has pointed out that Mrs. Robinson's concept of perfect competition is the equilibrium toward which the pure competition of Chamberlin would tend in the absence of any disturbing elements.[4]

The concept of free competition of the classical school, at least in its abstract form, had ceased to reflect reality if it ever had done so. Mrs. Robinson and Chamberlin realized that imperfect knowledge, differentiated products, and oligopolistic structures had become an inevitable part of the system itself and that another economic theory was needed which would consider these elements as endogenous factors. The result was the imperfect competition of Mrs. Robinson and the monopolistic competition of Chamberlin.[5] Chamberlin stressed the importance of product differentiation, but he failed to analyze the process whereby products become differentiated. Consequently, his analysis was rendered stationary and deterministic.[6]

Another advance occurred when Keynes presented his General Theory.[7] His contribution consisted of making the role played by the government in economic life a kind of semi-endogenous variable. Nowadays, it is difficult to find a single economic model which would not consider the role of the government as an indispensable part of economic life.

Starting from the static analysis of Keynes, J. R. Hicks built his dynamic theory, postulating similar (Keynesian) relations among economic variables.[8] The outcome was dynamic economics, which is characterized by the assumption that man's behavior is regimented. A great number of prominent economists concur with dynamic economic analysis based on assumption of functional relationships among economic variables. Baumol, for one, has said that the type of analysis presented by Marx and Schumpeter does not appeal to him because they failed to build a deterministic system, i.e., they failed to make their respective analyses operational.[9]

Deterministic economic analysis is not suitable for the purpose of this study because it considers economic activity as including only variations in the quantity of inputs. It assumes organization and technology as constant, or changing at some postulated rate. Hicks, for example, was aware of the role of innovation in the process of economic growth; he even got his model of dynamic economics moving by assuming an innovation. Yet he analyzed economic processes by postulating that changes in technology and organization are external to the working of the system. This kind of dynamic theory cannot help us to penetrate into the impact which the changes in organization had on the performance of the Yugoslav economy. In addition, deterministic analysis is not suitable for this study because it falls short of our working definition of economic development – it fails to tell us anything about the process of wants creation. It assumes that the sources of want generation are essentially noneconomic and therefore belong to other sciences.

J. M. Clark extended economic analysis to the analysis of human wants. In this respect his analysis meant, from the point of view adopted in this study, a step ahead in the analysis of the process of economic development.[10] According to Clark human wants are subject to constant changes. They are of a dynamic nature, and, consequently, their potential structure can only be guessed by those who are producing for exchange. Hence, the composition of output lags behind the ever changing wants, and there is, accordingly, a danger of over- or underproduction of goods and services. Clark's contribution is that he did not assume wants as given or as changing at some postulated rate. He tried to correlate idle capacities and the dynamic nature of human wants. Yet he fell short of explaining the process of change in our wants.

Another group of economists (e.g., Galbraith, Schumpeter, and Solterer) have stressed the importance of the analysis of the mechanism of economic changes, rather than the changes per se.

Galbraith maintains that in the United States private wants have been largely satisfied and that the production of new goods and services for private consumption presupposes the artificial creation of new wants through such media as advertising and emulation.[11] In fact, Galbraith implies that private wants are not unlimited, i.e., it is possible for man to overcome the element of scarcity with respect to his private wants. Galbraith's argument was exposed to sharp criticism by Zebot,[12] who stressed that human wants are unlimited, that, in view of this, the element of scarcity will always be present, and that man is endowed with a sufficient degree of intellect to act rationally even under the heavy pressure of advertisements.

The limitlessness of human wants implies that we cannot know them all. If this is so, how are new wants created? This question was answered by Schumpeter, who said that economic analysis must always start from the satisfaction of wants, since they are at the end of all production, and the given economic situation at any time must be understood from this aspect. Yet innovations in the economic system do not as a rule take place in such a way that first new wants arise spontaneously in consumers and then the productive apparatus swings around through their pressure. "It is the producer who initiates economic change and consumers are educated by him if necessary." [13] For Schumpeter advertisement is not an artificial creation of wants. It is the medium necessary for the actualization of wants which the producer hopes either exist but are yet unsatisfied, or are potential wants.

Since potential wants can only be estimated by the producer, the attempt to satisfy them — the innovating action — must include an important element of uncertainty with respect to the outcome of the innovating action. The term "innovating action" is used because the satisfacion of what is believed to be a potential want calls for a change in the allocation of resources; it is not a routine activity.

For Schumpeter the problem of want creation and satisfaction is at the root of economic development. For him, economic activity involves a double variation, i.e., changes in technology and organization along with variations in the quantity of inputs. Consequently, his theory of economic change can provide an analytical framework for the study of the Yugoslav economy — organizational changes being the most remarkable feature of that economy.

In the Schumpeter theory the three main ingredients of economic development are: the freedom to innovate, the availability of economic power to innovate, and a system of sufficient incentives.

Freedom to innovate is not, according to Schumpeter, political freedom or freedom to own property. It is the freedom to change the allocation of resources according to the innovator's vision. A degree of this freedom must exist in every society. The subject of the analysis should accordingly be the scope of the freedom to innovate, and this calls, of course, for the analysis of the organization.

The concept of economic power is another ingredient of economic development. The freedom of the producer to manufacture television sets if they are in his opinion potentially wanted, and the freedom of the consumer to buy a set because he expects to derive a degree of utility from it, are in fact futile without the economic power whereby they can actualize their respective visions. This power may come from retained earnings, from bank credit, from take-home pay, from consumer credit, but whatever happens to be the origin of this power its meaning is the same: *the ability to act in the market.*

Marx was the first economist to have an explicit theory of economic power. For him it is the result of an accumulation of capital and expanded production. For Schumpeter, who based his whole theory on the concept of economic power, this power is the result of credit creation. In a masterly way Schumpeter expressed the difference between dynamic analysis using the concept of power and classical and neoclassical stationary analyses using the concept of purchasing power as a flow.* He wrote:

> I was trying to construct a theoretical model of the process of economic change in time, or perhaps more clearly, to answer the question of how the economic system generates the force which incessantly transforms it . . . the classics would have made exceptions for increases in population and in savings, but this would only introduce a change in the data of the system and not add any new phenomena. I felt strongly that this was wrong, and that there was a source of energy within the economic system which itself disrupts any equilibrium that might be attained. If this is so then there must be a purely economic theory of economic change . . . It was not clear to me at the outset what to the reader will perhaps be obvious at once, that this idea and this aim are exactly the same as the idea and the aim which underlie the economic teaching of Karl Marx. In fact, what distinguishes him from the economists of his own time and those who preceded him, was precisely a vision of economic revolution as a distinct process generated by the economic system itself.[14]

According to Galbraith the concept of economic power was made explicit in Marx, although the classicists were not unaware of it. However, he says, both Marx and the classicists missed its importance and wanted

*Schumpeter did not mean to say that classical economists had not been aware of the concept of power. Adam Smith had the notion of power, but he had no theory of economic development based on the concept of economic power. For Smith monopolies were evils — and understandably so because the monopolies he talked about were mercantilist, politically established and sheltered monopolies. The monopolies Marx and Schumpeter talked about were of a different kind. These monopolies grew through their success in the market.

to eliminate it. The classicists did so through the concept of competition, while Marx envisaged its elimination in the final stage of communism. Marx's advantage was that he had a theory of power, which enabled him to elaborate on the development of capitalism. Still, owing to his concept of a superstructure shaped by the economic base, Marx was led to believe that the accumulation of power in the hands of capitalists would increase without limit. This belief was wrong, Galbraith says, because the democratic form of government in the West assured the workers their right to organize and to have power of their own. Galbraith defines economic power as the power of economic decision.[15]

Solterer broadened Schumpeter's concepts of the freedom to innovate and economic power. While Schumpeter concentrated on the analysis of producers' actions, assuming that they will carry out only those actions which they believe will satisfy some potential wants and which are in turn backed by a favorable income distribution, Professor Solterer included consumers in the concept of innovation whenever they act in a nonroutine manner in the market.[16] For example, when du Pont innovated nylon its managers had a vision that nylon would satisfy some potential wants and that the prevailing income distribution would enable those who wanted nylon to buy it. Solterer agrees, but he says that nylon was a new and untried product; therefore the consumers who wanted it could not estimate the utility they would derive from it. Even in the realm of analytical abstractions it would not be possible to calculate the marginal utility of nylon in terms of money. Hence there is, according to Solterer, an element of nonroutine behavior marked with uncertainty about the outcome in the consumer's activities in the market.

The Solterer concept of economic power[17] is also broader than Schumpeter's. Schumpeter dealt primarily with credit creation, extended to the producer and helping him to change the allocation of resources. For Solterer consumers' loans are a form of economic power as well. They provide consumers with the ability to carry out their vision with respect to the expected utility of their purchases. Undoubtedly credits extended to the consumer can affect the allocation of resources in the economy as a whole.

It could be claimed that the economic power of Schumpeter and Solterer is merely the old concept of purchasing power. However, the differences between the concept of purchasing power in classical and neoclassical economists and the concept of economic power in Marx,

Schumpeter, Galbraith, and Solterer are both qualitative and quantitative.

As to the qualitative differences, the purchasing power in classical and neoclassical analysis is a flow. There is an equilibrium solution for the system. Purchasing power, whether it is income to buy goods and services, retained profits, or new credit, is money available for carrying out exchanges within the closed system; it is a medium of exchange maximizing the marginal utilities of those who perform the acts of exchange. Economic power in the analyses of Marx, Schumpeter, Galbraith, and Solterer means the energy which disrupts this equilibrium relationship in the market. Physically it can be the same sum of money, but its use is different—it aims at the satisfaction of wants whose marginal utilities are not known and can be only anticipated. Here the same physical quantity performs a qualitatively different task; it is not a medium of exchange in a deterministic sense but the source of energy which disrupts and changes the equilibrium relationships. Instead of a flow it becomes the motor of economic development. Hicksian and similar analyses do not need this power. For in their mechanical dynamic models the process of creation of wants does not appear to be the main feature of economic development.

As to the quantitative differences, the concept of economic power is wider than the concept of purchasing power because it includes all other nonfinancial means whereby the innovator, be he consumer, producer, or state, can implement his vision.

To explain this concept diagrammatically, we recall the analysis in Chapter II, where it was said that a society is faced with the problem of determining the basic division of its gross national product between consumption and investment. Figure 3 (p. 51) illustrates the basic difference between a free-market economy and a centrally planned economy, emphasizing that the solution for both economies should be expected to be somewhere between the points of minimum (A) and maximum (B) investment. But why not at point A?

Assume a free-market economy in which all exchanges are done at margin.* As time goes on and no external factors influence economic

*By exchange at margin I mean a "marginal school postulate" of equilibrium relationship: (1) When marginal profit with respect to labor equals zero and equals marginal physical product of labor times price of the product minus tax—i.e., $MPP_1 \times P_x$ $(1 - t)$ equals price of labor. (2) When marginal profit with respect to capital equals zero equals $MPP_r \times P_x$ $(1 - t)$ equals price of capital.

processes net investments will approach zero, because all factors will be getting back from the total product the amounts equal to their respective marginal contributions. Economic power, in the context of marginal analysis, becomes zero, because all individuals and all enterprises adjust their expenditures in such a way that the last dollar they spend brings equal returns. Economic life will flow through time undisturbed because there is no *power* to disrupt equilibrium relationships from *inside* the system. Hence, assuming the absence of external disturbances, the social indifference-preference map will be such that the highest indifference curve attainable is tangent to the maximum production curve at point A. Classical and neoclassical analyses could not explain, except by introducing external factors, why the point of tangency lies above point A. Therefore, they are, in fact, more stationary than dynamic, analyzing the results of economic changes rather than the process of change.

The Schumpeter theory provides an answer to why the point of tangency is above point A (*external factors* remaining constant). Herein lies the meaning of economic power. It is the energy which originates from within the economic system, disrupts marginal equilibrium relationships, and diverts resources from their routine uses for the purpose of using them to satisfy some potential wants. When resources are diverted from their routine uses, net investment becomes positive and the point of tangency moves up. In a free enterprise economy this diversion of the resources comes about by the individual actions of potential entrepreneurs seeking greater profits. In a centrally planned economy the diversion occurs through the direct administrative policy of the government.

The third ingredient of economic development is the system of incentives. Why should one try to implement his vision and break the established equilibrium relationships unless he is given sufficient incentives for the risk he takes? For the producer the risk is that his vision of some potential wants may prove wrong. For the consumer the risk is that he will derive less than the expected utility from the particular good or serv-

---

This same relationship can also be stated as $\Pi$ maximum when

$$\Delta\Pi/\Delta L = 0 = MPP_l \times P_x\ (1-t) - P_1, \text{ and also when}$$
$$\Delta\Pi/\Delta K = 0 = MPP_r \times P_x\ (1-t) - P_r,$$

where $MPP_1$ = marginal physical product of labor, $P_x$ = product, t = tax rate, $P_1$ = price of labor, $P_r$ = price of capital.

ice he bought. For the state this risk may be an increased tension in society.

The whole problem of economic development, once the Schumpeter theory is adopted, boils down to the problem of finding the right organization within which opportunities and incentives for innovating actions are maximized.[18] There is no blueprint for the best organization. To propose it would mean the imposition of another deterministic model. Each country, because of its history, geography, level of culture, and political system, would probably find its most convenient organizational framework to be different from that of others. This approach does not deny the importance of such economic instruments as fiscal policies, monetary policies, and the rate and pattern of investment. But it stresses the enormous importance of the organization for fast and successful economic development. Within the framework of its political system the U.S.S.R. could probably organize the structure of its economy in a number of different ways. The problem, then, is to analyze not merely the economic instruments used for the attainment of planned goals but the organization of the economy and its impact on the three ingredients of economic development. There is always room to reshape the structure of a national economy within the framework of the same political system. It is true, of course, that political arrangements have their economic implications, but it should always be possible for the government of a country to choose one from among a few alternative economic organizations, each alternative having its origin in the country's sociopolitical arrangement.

In order to verify that Schumpeter's theory of economic development provides a meaningful analytical explanation of the significance of organizational innovations in Yugoslavia, we must review these innovations with respect to their impact on the three basic ingredients of economic development: the freedom to innovate, the availability of economic power to innovate, and the adequacy of the system of incentives. In fact, the analysis so far has provided the ground for asserting that the Schumpeter scheme is helpful in assessing the performance of the Yugoslav economy: the rate of economic growth changed after each major innovating action – it decreased in the late 1940's, it went up after 1953, and again after 1961–62; each major innovation was followed by a cluster of smaller innovating actions; and each major innovation primarily influenced the pattern of investment.

*The Freedom to Innovate.* The Yugoslav economic plan before the announced innovation of 1950–51 was similar to the Soviet economic plan. The complete failure of the First Five Year Plan contributed to the decision of the government to change its system of planning. However, the failure of this economic plan was not the only cause which set off the major organizational innovation of the early 1950's. Tito himself stated on a number of occasions that the system of tight administrative planning had had bad effects on the social life of the country in general and therefore had to be abolished.[19] In the early 1950's Edvard Kardelj, now president of the Federal Parliament, became the most ardent promoter of the new economic system. From his speeches and writings it appears that he considers the rise of bureaucracy one of the greatest potential dangers a socialist country has to face. Kardelj's attacks on the bureaucratic apparatus of the state triggered a number of studies of this problem. Jovan Djordjevich, the chairman of the board of legal advisors to the Federal Government, wrote that the leading opponents of bureaucratic control in socialist countries have been Lenin and Kardelj.[20] Uvalich wrote that there is always a danger that bureaucracy may degenerate and he called on the Workers' Councils to resist and fight bureaucratic tendencies.[21]

Because of the failure of the First Five Year Plan, the bad social effects of the production plan, and the political showdown between Stalin and Tito, the Yugoslav government was forced to admit that it is impossible to calculate the outcome of all economic activities and actions with the exactness of mathematics. As a result of this "realization," the Yugoslav economic plan adopted the language of "anticipations" (see Ch. II). "Anticipations" imply, of course, nonfunctional relationships among economic variables, i.e., the acceptance of the concept of subjective time in the process of economic planning.* The present system of economic planning in Yugoslavia determines the amount of autonomous investment and its allocation among different industries, and that is as far as the plan goes. The microeconomic decisions within each industry are, in general, left to the market mechanism.

The change from a deterministic to a relatively indeterministic system

* The subjective concept of time is a period of time dependent on the action of the actor. In other words, free action of man and random elements are capable of influencing the sequence of events. The subjective concept of time in economics was developed by G. Shackle, in one of his finest monographs, *Time and Economics* (Amsterdam: North-Holland, 1958).

of planning has increased the scope of freedom to innovate in Yugoslavia. There is still an element of administrative determinism with respect to the macroeconomic decisions in the Yugoslav system of economic planning, but at the same time the *existing* firms in Yugoslavia are free to change (within the framework of their legally chartered activities) their production functions in accordance with their vision of the results of their innovating actions.

*The Availability of Economic Power to Innovate.* Before the change in the system of economic planning in the early 1950's, the banking system in Yugoslavia served as an intermediary organ of the government, channeling funds to and from the firm in accordance with the predetermined financial plan. The firm, even assuming it had freedom to innovate, could not hope to get funds for carrying out an unplanned action. After 1950–51, and even more after the actual implementation of the second innovation in 1953, the banking system in Yugoslavia had the power to provide means to enterprises for carrying out unplanned actions, provided that their expected profitabilities were high relative to those of competing projects. In addition, the banks obtained the right to extend their own credits to firms subject to the reserve requirement regulations.

The power of the banking system to effectuate the ultimate allocation of funds on the microeconomic level puts the banks in a position of heavy responsibility.* The banking system in Yugoslavia is responsible for providing as harmonious an interaction between the administrative macroeconomic decisions and the market-oriented microeconomic decisions as possible. For the banks to achieve the best distribution of funds among productive units, two conditions have to be satisfied: The officials responsible for making decisions must possess strong personal characters and they have to be able to apply economic analysis. No data are available concerning the first factor, but it is safe to assume that personal connections in Yugoslavia play an important role. With respect to the second factor, Djordje Peklich [22] has complained that many deficiencies in banking in Yugoslavia today are due to the fact that only 2.3 per cent of all bank employees have a B.A. degree or better. At the same

*It is, of course, possible that the banks may find themselves unable to loan out the sum total of money from the G.I.F. allocated to some economic branches for lack of demand. Were such a situation to arise, the annual social plan provides that unused funds can be shifted to some other uses, subject to approval by the Federal Government.

time the innovation of 1961 indicates a continued rise in the importance of the banking system.

In an article on the role of credits in the Yugoslav economy Professor Vuckovich [23] emphasized that the ability of the banks to extend credit is essential in a developing economy like Yugoslavia's. Edvard Kardelj uses almost every opportunity to stress the importance of the banking system. In 1960 he began proclaiming that the time had come for an increased emphasis on monetary policies. He seems to believe that an increased reliance on monetary policies would increase the importance of purely economic criteria and decrease the influence of bureaucracy.*

The conclusion is evident. The rising importance of the banking system since the early 1950's has continuously increased the ability of the Yugoslav firm to carry out innovating (unplanned) actions.

*The System of Incentives.* When the Yugoslav government changed the system of planning and abolished the system of production quotas in the early 1950's, the important problem of making leisure expensive in terms of work was solved by introducing into the economy a new system of incentives based on differentiated earnings for different success in the market. The result was a rise in the importance of Workers' Councils and also an ever increasing degree of correlation between the wage fund of the Yugoslav firm and its profits.

Schumpeter's theory of economic changes seems to provide a clear in-

*"The carrying out of such tasks will enable us to take further steps to consolidate the material basis of social-self-government. I am thinking primarily of the need for the gradual substitution of fiscal methods of forming centralized funds for a suitable credit and banking system. This will make it possible not only to overcome the many difficulties in the present technique of distribution among the working collectives and the community, but also to ensure that the administering of economic funds is really based on objective economic principles. Today, these funds are still subject to the interference and subjective criteria of different political and other social factors, and even ordinary amateurism.

"I think that this will be a great step towards the decentralization of economic-administrative functions and social self-management. By following this path, we shall also considerably reduce the pressure of such detrimental tendencies as the formation of enterprises without sound economic calculation, etc., as well as the tendency for the indispensable centralization of economic funds to be effected spontaneously, through enterprises of separate economic associations and their funds, instead of being effected within the social plan, through the corresponding social mechanism. Such a system would also make it possible to increase substantially the independence and responsibility of the republics for the material and social development of their respective territories, which is essential for the sound development of the Yugoslav socialist community as a whole" (Kardelj, "The Position of Working People in the Conditions of Self-Management," *International Affairs* (Belgrade), December 5, 1961, p. 14).

sight into the reasons for the economic stagnation before 1953 – this, we recall, was the period of centralized planning, when strict limitations were imposed on the scope of the three basic ingredients of economic development; the rapid economic growth after 1953 – when the innovation of 1950–51 was in fact implemented and the scope of the three ingredients of economic development increased; and another increase in the rate of economic growth in 1963 – when the results of the 1961 innovation began to be reaped.

The link between the rate of economic growth in Yugoslavia and the pattern of organizational changes which was observed earlier in this study can now be analytically explained and utilized for policy suggestions and evaluations with respect to future changes in the Yugoslav economic system.

# VI SUMMARY

THE "Yugoslav experiment" has made several contributions to the static economic theory of socialism. Analysis of the Yugoslav economy suggests that one of its most important facets is the attempt to solve the problem of the interaction of macroeconomic and microeconomic decisions; macroeconomic decisions are, in general, administratively imposed, while microeconomic decisions tend to be based on the market mechanism. We must say "tend to" because the microeconomic decisions only approach a conformation to the working of the market, since administrative interferences by local governments diminish the potential impact of the market mechanism in Yugoslavia. The solution of the interaction of politically administered macro-measures and market-induced micro-decisions has been entrusted to the banking system. The Federal Government orders the basic distribution of scarce resources and expects the banks to make the most of it. While the Federal Government retains its power to decide, administratively, the size of funds available for, say, the shoe industry and for the production of steel, it asks the banks to see that these administratively allocated funds are then distributed within each industry strictly in accordance with market principles of profitability. In other words, the Federal Government does not care very much whether the money allocated to the shoe industry is used to further research or to produce brown or black shoes; it wants, first, to control the percentages of the General Investment Fund going into various industries, and second, to be assured that within each industry the funds are used as effectively as possible. The result has been the growing importance of monetary and fiscal policies in Yugoslavia.

On the assumption that the Federal Government's scale of preferences with respect to the allocation of resources is different from that of the citizens, the rigid planning on the macro-level tends to distort the flow of economic life. The micro-decisions, on the other hand, tend to distribute the supply of loanable funds allocated to each industry in accordance with the scale of consumers' preferences in relation to the products of that industry. It is obvious that the market-induced distribution of funds within each industry can only minimize, but not eliminate, the distortions in the allocation of resources caused by the macro-decisions of the government. The attempt to solve the interaction of macro- and micro-decisions through the banking system as a kind of intermediary institution is a definite contribution to the static economic theory of socialism.

The important shortcoming of the contemporary static economic theory of socialism is that it cannot give socialist economies any insight into the problem of how to achieve the maximum productive contribution from resources once their allocation is determined. This problem arises because of the disparity between the planned allocation of resources and the allocation of resources which the individual citizen would prefer. This misallocation of resources is bound to diminish incentives to work and to increase the relative value of leisure. Consequently, only less than the full effort of all factors of production can be expected. The Yugoslav economy has made yet another contribution to the economic theory of socialism with respect to this problem. It has shown a method by which a socialist economy may introduce a strong incentive to work better and harder. The incentive, derived by paying the employees of enterprises from the net profits of their respective enterprises, induces employees to exercise the maximum effort to assure themselves of higher incomes. The 6 per cent tax on the capital assets of the enterprise tends to impel the management to use both fixed and circulating capital as efficiently as possible. Incentives in this category are an offsetting factor to the negative incentives associated with the inherent disparity between the prevailing planning preferences and the spontaneous preferences of the people themselves.

How important it is for the static economic theory of socialism to solve the problem of efficient utilization of scarce resources can be observed from the Yugoslav economy. There we have only to compare the productivity of labor and capital, which are given profit incentives, with the productivity of farmers, who are not given any incentives to work harder and better.

With respect to the dynamic economic theory of socialism, the Yugoslav experiment seems to justify reliance on Schumpeter's theory of economic development. The analysis of the process of organizational changes and the performance of the Yugoslav economy indicates a rather close relationship between changes in the three ingredients of economic development and the rate of economic growth. True, we could not establish causal relationship, since the period of time under consideration is limited. But the following working hypothesis can be proposed: change in the freedom, the ability, and/or the incentives to innovate has had a definite impact on the rate of economic growth in Yugoslavia. This working hypothesis suggests that the Schumpeter theory of economic development can be used for an analytical explanation of dynamic changes in the Yugoslav economy. It provides a useful analytical tool for an evaluation of economic changes in Yugoslavia.

On the grounds of the working hypothesis and given the political system in Yugoslavia, the most important task of the economy seems to be an attempt to improve the efficiency of the banking system.

Finally, the working hypothesis has one other far-reaching implication: the freer man becomes in the pursuit of his material and spiritual wants, and the more incentives he is given to pursue his wants, the more he will use his creative abilities. And we know from Schumpeter, and from similar observations of the correlation between human incentives and economic systems, that the greater the exercise of man's will and intellect in the field of economic life is, the higher is the rate of economic growth. From the analysis it appears that the Yugoslav experiment has increased the scope of freedom to innovate and has supplied incentives to innovate since 1953. So, from a historical perspective, the Yugoslav government has been enabling its citizens to realize their visions and to use their creative abilities.

# Appendixes

# *Appendix I. KARL MARX AND THE PROBLEM OF TRANSITION FROM CAPITALISM TO SOCIALISM*

THE purpose of this appendix is to establish, on purely analytical grounds, the conditions necessary and sufficient for the transition from capitalism to socialism in Marx's scheme of socioeconomic progress. To underline the point, I shall not attempt to adjudge the validity of Marx's scheme of human progress, my task being the analysis of the conditions which according to his scheme—taken merely as an analytical proposition—must be present prior to the imposition of socialism.

I shall first establish the meaning of Marx's "scientific socialism" and then derive a few criteria for checking the proper timing for imposing "scientific socialism." These criteria will help establish the applicability or inapplicability of Marx's scheme to the socioeconomic conditions prevailing in a country prior to the imposition of socialism.

From his vision[1] of the process of change, Karl Marx predicted that in the process of economic development the law of diminishing returns will be more than offset by organizational and technological innovations, and that the future of mankind does not harbor some kind of economic stagnation as predicted by Ricardo, Malthus, and other classical economists.[2] In 1884, Friedrich Engels pointed out the main fault of classical

1. For a fuller understanding of the meaning and significance of the concept of vision, I quote Joseph Schumpeter: "perception of a set of related phenomena is a prescientific act. It must be performed in order to give to our minds something to do scientific work on — to indicate an object of research — but it is not scientific in itself. But though prescientific, it is not preanalytic. It does not simply consist in perceiving facts by one or more of our senses. These facts must be recognized as having some meaning or relevance that justifies our interest in them and they must be recognized as related . . . This mixture of perceptions and prescientific analysis we shall call the research worker's vision . . ." Later in the same article, Schumpeter says that vision is the prerequisite for any scientific work. "No new departure in any science is possible without it. Through it we acquire new material for our scientific endeavors and something to formulate, to defend, to attack" ("Science and Ideology," *American Economic Review*, March 1949, pp. 350, 359).

2. Marx, *Philosophical and Economic Manuscripts of 1844* (Moscow: Foreign Languages Publishing House, 1960), p. 109.

economics: it neglects the importance of technological innovation. In the *Outlines of a Critique of Political Economy*, he wrote: "Malthus puts forward a calculation upon which his whole system is based. Population increases in a geometrical progression . . . the productive power of the land increases in arithmetical progression . . . but . . . where has it been proved that the productivity of the land increases in arithmetic progression? The area of land is limited—that is perfectly true. But . . . even if we assume that the increase of output associated with this increase of labor is not always proportionate to the latter, there still remains a third element—which the economist . . . never considers . . . [that is,] science, the progress of which is just as limitless and at least as rapid as that of population." On the contrary, mankind is to experience enormous development in productive forces culminating eventually in the subordination of nature to man. This last stage in development of the human race when man subjects nature to his complete control Marx called a higher phase of communist society.[3]

From Hegel Marx borrowed the concept of dialectics,[4] but he moved Hegel's concept of progress from the sphere of ideas to the material world[5] of Feuerbach. This is how the concept of dialectical materialism was born.[6] The concept of dialectical materialism has, according to Stalin, four postulates: (1) All things should be considered in their interconnection. (2) All things should be considered in their process of evolution. (3) The process of development is to be understood and analyzed as the process of qualitative change. (4) "Internal contradictions are inherent in all things and phenomena of nature . . . the process of development . . . takes place . . . as a 'struggle of opposite tendencies.'" The use of dialectical materialism to "explain" the development of human societies is historical materialism—that is, an application of Marx's philosophy to the study of socioeconomic changes.[7]

3. Marx, "Critique of the Gotha Program," *Marx and Engels, Basic Writings on Politics and Philosophy*, ed. Lewis Feuer (Garden City, N.Y.: Doubleday, 1959), p. 119.

4. For Marx and Engels dialectics is the comprehension of things "in their essential connection . . . motion, origin, and ending . . . Nature works dialectically and not metaphysically; that she does not move in the eternal oneness of a perpetually recurring circle, but goes through a real historical evolution" (Engels, *Socialism, Utopian and Scientific* (Moscow: Foreign Languages Publishing House, 1946), p. 63).

5. The basic issue between Hegel and Marx — and for that matter between materialist and idealist — had been What comes first, spirit or matter? Hegel would say that spirit is prior to matter. Marx, on the other hand, would say that matter comes first; the origin of materialism Marx traced to England, and in particular to Bacon. See Marx and Engels, *Die Heilige Familie* (Frankfurt A.M., 1845), pp. 201–204.

6. See Joseph V. Stalin, *Dialectical and Historical Materialism* (Moscow: 1941), pp. 5–9.

7. See Engels, *Socialism, Utopian and Scientific*, pp. 94–95.

For Marx the process of economic development consists of a series of quantitative and small qualitative changes culminating in a large qualitative change—a new socioeconomic system—which moves mankind a step closer to communism. Marx's statement of this point reads: "At a certain state of their development the material forces of production in society come into conflict with the existing relations of production, or, what is but a legal expression for the same thing, with the property relations within which they had been at work before. From forms of development of the forces of production these relations turn into their fetters. Then comes the period of social revolution. With the change of the economic foundation the entire immense superstructure is more or less rapidly transformed. In considering such transformation the distinction should always be made between the material transformation of the economic conditions of production which can be determined with the precision of natural science, and the legal, political, aesthetic, or ideological forms in which man becomes conscious of this conflict and fights it out. Just as our opinion of an individual is not based on what he thinks of himself, so can we not judge such a period of transformation by its own consciousness; on the contrary, this consciousness must rather be explained from the contradictions of material life, from the existing conflict between the social forces of production and the relations of production."[8]

This quotation comprises the most significant vision of Karl Marx: a gradual accumulation of quantitative and qualitative changes (growth of productive forces and concentration of capital), then increased tension in society when the existing institutions fetter the further development of productive forces, and, finally, emergence of a new social organization.[9]

8. "A Contribution to the Critique of Political Economy," *Marx and Engels, Basic Writings on Politics and Philosophy*, pp. 43–44.

9. I shall mention only three economists who supported either explicitly (Schumpeter and Solterer) or implicitly (Fellner) Marx's vision of the process of development but not his conclusions and predictions concerning the sequence of events. "When looking at economic theory from the point of view of structure we may see an increasing awareness that economic activity involves a double variation. Classical economic theory, by its harmony postulate, fixes the structure of action . . . General equilibrium theory in its present . . . form of input-output analysis has again only one type of variation, the quantity of inputs, since the structure of the economy considered is taken as a datum. Marxist theory has a double variation . . . Marxist awareness of double variation . . . refers only to the evolutionary stages and disappears in . . . communism" (Joseph Solterer, "Structure of a Pluralistic Economy," *Review of Social Economy*, March 1956, pp. 15–16). "Classical thinking did not rely . . . enough on the ability of . . . economies to bring forth adequate technological and organizational progress" William Fellner, *Modern Economic Analysis* (New York: McGraw-Hill, 1960), p. 87. For Joseph Schumpeter's views, see his preface to the Japanese edition of the *Theory of Economic Development*.

To reach the final state of affluence mankind must pass through definite types of "relations of production," each of them being an inevitable and unavoidable feature of the economic history of mankind on its long journey to communism.[10] Every set of "relations of production" has its place in human progress toward ultimate affluence, and should not leave the scene before its historical contribution to the progress of mankind has been fully utilized.

Marx never failed to recognize the historical necessity for capitalism. For example, I quote from the *Communist Manifesto* overlooked by many economists in their eagerness to condemn Marx: "The bourgeoisie . . . has been the first to show what man's activity can bring about. It has accomplished wonders far surpassing Egyptian pyramids, Roman aqueducts, and Gothic Cathedrals; it has conducted expeditions that put in the shade all former exoduses of nations and crusades . . . The bourgeoisie cannot exist without constantly revolutionizing the instruments of production and thereby relations of production, and with them the whole relations of society . . . The bourgeoisie, by the rapid improvements of production, by the immensely facilitated means of communications, draws all, even the most barbarial nations into civilization. The cheap prices of its commodities are the heavy artillery with which it batters down all Chinese walls . . . The bourgeoisie during its rule of scarce one hundred years has created more massive and more colossal productive forces than have all preceding generations together."[11] To this Schumpeter said that all "the achievements referred to are attributed to the bourgeoisie alone which is more than any thoroughly bourgeois economist would claim."[12]

The particular set of the relations of production which is to succeed capitalism after that stage has performed its historical function Engels termed "scientific socialism."[13]

Engels wanted to draw a line between the preference for socialism and the scientific analysis of it. He said: "To all [French and English socialists and the earlier German communists] socialism is the expression of absolute truth, reason, and justice, and has only to be discovered to conquer all the world by virtue of its own power. And as absolute truth is independent of time, space, and of the historical development

10. There are five stages that, according to Marx, the human race has to live through before it reaches the final stage, Communism — primitive society, slavery, feudal society, capitalism, socialism. Obviously, Marx took European history (of his time) as the basis for his prophecies. A similar error underlines Rostow's analysis of the process of economic growth. See Walter Rostow, *The Stages of Economic Growth* (Cambridge University Press, 1961), and Cyril Zebot, *Economics of Competitive Coexistence* (New York: Praeger, 1964).

11. Marx and Engels, *The Communist Manifesto* (Chicago: Regnery, 1954), pp. 19–23.

12. *Capitalism, Socialism and Democracy* (New York: Harper, 1950), p. 7.

13. *Socialism, Utopian and Scientific*, pp. 74–75 and 92–93.

of man, it is a mere accident when and where it is discovered . . . To make a science of socialism, it had first to be placed upon a real basis . . . for this it was necessary, (1) to present the capitalist method of production in its historical connection and its inevitableness during a particular historical period, and therefore, also to present its inevitable downfall; and (2) to lay bare its essential character . . . This was done by the discovery of surplus-value . . . These two great discoveries, the materialistic concept of history and the revolution of the secret of capitalist production through surplus-value, we owe to Marx. With these discoveries socialism became a science."

Marx and Engels considered "scientific socialism" as a transitory stage between capitalism and pure communism.[14] Scientific socialism, like any other socioeconomic system, has a set of tasks to perform before its useful life is over. We gather from Marx's and Engels's writings that they allocated to scientific socialism two broad functions: (1) to accelerate further development of productive forces, and (2) to deal with those remnants of capitalism that outlived it.[15]

Marx's scheme is a deterministic one because he considers all relations among the variables involved in the process of economic change as being functional and the outcome as a calculable and predictable event. Marx excludes both random elements and the free action of man as factors capable of causing economic changes. There seems to be an element of stoicism in Marx: one social system will succeed the previous one at the right time and independently of man's will. And the right time will come only after "the productive forces for which there is room in [the old society] have been [fully] developed, and new, higher relations of production never appear before the material conditions of their existence have matured in the womb of the old society."

If one were to imagine a state in which Marxian socialism was somehow imposed before capitalism had a chance to develop, the imposition of scientific socialism in the "impatient" state could be caused by a number of things: injustices,[16] foreign interferences, internal revolution com-

14. See Marx, *Critique of the Gotha Programma*, pp. 44–45.

15. Marx, *Critique of the Gotha Programma*, p. 29. Engels, *Socialism, Utopian and Scientific*, pp. 126–127. Engels's letter to Bebel of March 18, 1875 ("As long as the proletariat still needs the state, it needs it not in the interests of freedom, but for the purpose of [crushing] its antagonists.").

16. It should not be forgotten that people who often would not be ready to fight over philosophical ideas and economic models may quickly do so because of social and material exploitation. It is outside the scope of this paper to analyze the reasons for the success of, say, the Chinese or Cuban revolutions, but it is not an exaggeration to state that social and material injustices which existed in these countries prior to the revolution helped Mao Tse-Tung and Castro far more than did Karl Marx's ideas.

By "injustice" I mean interference by any power with what is considered at each economic and cultural stage of social development a fair distribution of

bined with foreign interference, a belief that Marx's scheme offers a better opportunity and environment for rapid economic development than free competition, and so forth. Imposition of scientific socialism by any of these causes makes the sequence of events deviate from the Marxian deterministic scheme. The time of imposition of scientific socialism appears to depend on man's will and/or random elements, another way of saying that scientific socialism is imposed in the impatient state by deviating from the objective concept of time of Karl Marx.

At this point one must, however, do justice to Marx. Marx believed in man and in his creative ability probably more than any other economist in the nineteenth century. He wrote, "Men make their own history," and "The materialist doctrines [are] that men are products of circumstances and upbringing, and that, therefore, changed men are products of other circumstances . . . The coincidence of the changing circumstances and of human activity can be conceived and rationally understood only as revolutionary practice."[17] However, Marx limited the ability of man to exercise his creative ability. He subordinated man and his consciousness to class consciousness and to the stage of development of the productive forces. Hence, man's action reflects class consciousness, in turn, formed (preconditioned) by the material conditions of production.

The basic difference between Marx's scientific socialism and the one imposed in the impatient state is obvious. Marx's scheme is a deterministic one: scientific socialism is to emerge from the womb of capitalism at a certain state of development of productive forces – neither sooner nor later – and its emergence is independent of man's will, except for delays in adjustment of superstructure to the new mode of production. But the imposition of scientific socialism in the impatient state is not conditioned and timed by natural laws independent of man's will.

Scientific socialism in the impatient state faces social and economic problems different from those of Marx's timely scientific socialism. In the impatient state the new relations of production are imposed upon the society before the conditions that would naturally bring about those new relations of production have arisen. The problem of the impatient state is not one of adjusting the relations of production to the requirements set by the degree of development of the productive forces, but one of bringing the productive forces into agreement with the new relations of production. This is Marx's scheme upside down.

---

national product. The distortion of fair distribution not only causes an increased tension among the people but also tends to diminish their productive efforts. To substitute work for leisure, man must have incentives. A distorted fair distribution of income diminishes the incentives to work hard and tends to raise the relative value of leisure.

17. Marx, "Theses on Feuerbach," *Marx and Engels, Basic Writings on Politics and Philosophy*, p. 244.

I shall use the term "premature scientific socialism" for Marx's socialism whenever it is imposed before the objective requirements set by Marx and Engels for it.

How can one assert that scientific socialism in the impatient state, or, for that matter, in any other state, has been imposed prematurely, especially since neither Marx nor Engels said much about the precise timing of the transformation? Because the transformation would take place at the historically predetermined time, they considered any attempt to prophesy it unwarranted and a waste of energy.[18]

It is possible, however, to derive from Marx's own writings some criteria to help assess the validity of claims by rulers of any country that they are building the scientific socialism of Karl Marx. To do so one has to understand two crucial Marxian concepts, "relations of production" and "productive forces."

"Relations of production" I shall define as relations among men in the process of production. Through the history of mankind before the final stage is reached, these relations of production are relations among aliens; private property causes this alienation of man from man.[19]

18. Marx and Engels were actively engaged in politics, and this fact should explain their repeated assessment, first in 1848 and then in 1875, that the time for the transformation had come. See their *Communist Manifesto,* pp. 24–25; and Engels's *Socialism, Utopian and Scientific,* pp. 131–132.

19. The concept of "alienated labor" was the object of Marx's analysis in his first manuscript, written in 1844. Marx pointed out some of the shortcomings of classical political economy: "Political economy begins with the fact of private property; it does not explain it. It conceives the material process of private property, as this occurs in reality, in general, and abstracts formulas which then serve it as laws. It does not comprehend these laws; that is, it does not show how they arise out of the nature of private property . . . the only moving forces which political economy recognizes are avarice and the war between the avaricious competition" ("Economic and Philosophical Manuscripts of 1844," *Marx's Concept of Man,* ed. Erich Fromm (New York: Ungar, 1961), pp. 93–94).

Marx's analysis of the concept of alienated labor consists of four successive steps: (1) Since it does not belong to him, the product of his labor appears to the worker as an *alien object.* (2) Consequently, the worker considers his work as "imposed, *forced labor.* It is not the satisfaction of a need, but only a *means* for satisfying other needs. This is the relationship of the worker to his own activity as something alien and not belonging to him" (*ibid.,* pp. 98–99). (3) "Conscious life activity distinguishes man from the life activity of animals . . . Alienated labor reverses the relationship, in that man because he is a self-conscious being makes his life actively, his *being,* only a *means* for his *existence* . . . Thus alienated labor turns the species life of man . . . into an *alien* being and into a *means* for his *individual* existence. It alienates . . . his human life" (*ibid.,* pp. 101–103). (4) "A direct consequence of the alienation of man from the product of his labor, from his life activity and from his species life is that *man is alienated* from other men" (*ibid.,* p. 103). From these considerations about the alienated labor stems the final conclusion concerning the nature of private property: "Private property is . . . the product . . . of alienated labor, of the external relations of the worker to nature and to himself" (*ibid.,* pp. 105–109).

The existence of classes in society as a consequence of the alienation of man from man led Marx to conclude that relations among men in the process of production are characterized by incessant class struggle. And conversely, since, according to Marx, there are basically two distinct classes in each society until the stage of affluence is attained, the fight among mutual aliens takes the form of class struggle.

As the social system grows toward its maturity, the class struggle within it intensifies. Marx's scheme gives two basic reasons for this: (1) the process of polarization among in-between classes accelerates in the maturing system, and (2) the relations of production at some point start fettering the productive forces. Finally the old system breaks down, and the new one, with a qualitatively different set of relations of production, emerges from the womb of the old. The intensity of the class struggle within the society is thus the first criterion for judging the correct timing of the imposition of scientific socialism.

The intensity of the class struggle is not open to cardinal measurement, but one can ascertain it in a particular country by observing national history, social philosophy, and political life, the development of socialist thought, and any other factor which would seem pertinent. These observations — of both the different aspects of the social life in the country and their changing historical content — should uncover the strength of class consciousness among the members of the society and, consequently, the intensity of the class struggle.

The second crucial concept in Marx's analysis of the process of socioeconomic change is the degree of development of the productive forces of society. The productive forces represent at each moment of time the relation between man and nature in the production of the necessities of life. In the concept of productive forces Marx included technology, stock of capital on hand, labor force, working habits, and education. The stress on working habits and education shows another qualitative difference between the Marxian and classical schools. Marx sensed the importance of technological development and believed that without appropriate increases in knowledge changes in the capital-labor ratio would eventually reach the point of saturation. Marx's vision of the need for education may be much like Schultz's "second puzzle," that in underdeveloped countries the amount of capital that can be efficiently used is limited because of the low educational standards.[20]

Incessant development of productive forces leads, according to Marx, toward accumulation and centralization of capital. Schumpeter considered the vision of the process of centralization of capital one of Marx's greatest contributions.[21] This accumulation and centralization of capital

20. Theodore Schultz, "Investment in Human Capital," *American Economic Review*, March 1961, pp. 1–17.

21. *Capitalism, Socialism and Democracy*, p. 31.

call for an organizational innovation capable of offsetting the law of diminishing returns. Marx erred in identifying major organizational innovation with a comprehensive social revolution; he did not take into account that existing institutions may adjust to the requirements of the developing productive forces within the broad framework of the existing relations of production. The major qualitative change, Marx believed, will always be introduced by means of social revolution, though it is true that he changed his views in later years. In his speech to the workers of Amsterdam in 1872, he declared that in different countries different degrees of development of productive forces will call for a social change that would not necessarily have to take place by means of revolution. He pointed out that in England and in the United States revolutions need not occur. It is possible that Bernstein and Kautsky drew their "revisionist" inspirations from this speech. The fact remains that Marx expected a comprehensive change in the capitalist relations of production to take place at some future date. When the change would occur would depend, however, not on the degree of development of the productive forces but on the relation between developing productive forces and the relations of production, i.e., on the relation between the rising ability to produce and the organizational framework within which the production takes place.

Earlier I noted that the relations of production in capitalism, according to Marx, are, in the main, the relations between the owners of capital and the workers. The means of life and existence for the workers is "labor power," which is the productive asset they own and have to sell in order to live. But they can sell their labor only if it brings surplus to the employer, i.e., if their work can be converted into money in the market. Hence, the very existence of the workers and the social and economic performance of the system depend ultimately upon the profit expectations of owners of capital at each moment of time. If for any reason profits were expected to decline, the ensuing unemployment, if protracted and increasing as a percentage of the labor force, would eventually bring about a qualitative organizational change, a new social system capable of reconciling the contradictions between the productive forces and their organizational framework. In Marx's scheme the development of the productive forces and the subsequent concentration of capital will have a tendency, once the honeymoon between the productive forces and the relations of production is over, to lower the average rate of profit and to increase the percentage of the labor force out of work. This unemployed reserve army, and not a Malthusian pressure of population, will keep wage rates down at the subsistence level.

The trend in the average rate of profit in conjunction with the percentage of the labor force unemployed is the second criterion for judging the correct "objective" timing of the imposition of Marx's scientific socialism.

The two criteria for judging the correct timing of the imposition of Marx's socialism are closely related, and neither of them, taken alone, is sufficient to answer the question whether the imposition of scientific socialism in a country has been premature or not.

Taking the Marxian scheme as an analytical proposition, I have set forth its determinism, i.e., a complete exclusion of random elements and the free action of man as possible influences on the sequence of events, and the objective conditions which not only must be present prior to the transition from capitalism to socialism but also are supposed to bring about this transition, independently of man's will.

From Marx's own writings I derived two criteria for judging the correlation between his deterministic scheme and empirical reality in a country. These two criteria are of universal validity in assessing—on purely Marxian grounds—the claim of any country to be engaged in building its socialism on Marxian foundations. True, the scope of these criteria is relatively narrow because they do not help either to reject or to approve the rise of socialism in a country, and they are not helpful in assessing the ultimate validity of the Marxian scheme of socioeconomic progress. They are helpful only in showing whether the rise of socialism in a country is at variance with the Marxian scheme of human progress.

# *Appendix II.* SCIENTIFIC SOCIALISM OF KARL MARX *vs.* SOCIALISM IN YUGOSLAVIA

IN THIS appendix I list a number of books, monographs, and articles that provide material sufficient to relate the two criteria derived in Appendix I to the socioeconomic conditions in Yugoslavia prior to World War II. The evidence available suggests that socioeconomic conditions in Yugoslavia in 1941 were at variance with the socioeconomic conditions expected to exist – according to the Marx scheme – in a country at the moment of its transition from capitalism to socialism. This, of course, neither denies nor approves the imposition of socialism in Yugoslavia.

With respect to the first criteria, the following readings should help establish whether the history of the southern Slavs reflects Marx's statement that "the history of all hitherto existing societies is the history of class struggle."[1] Also, the readings reflect the intensity of the class struggle between capitalists and the proletariat in Yugoslavia before 1941.

For the penetration of the southern Slavs into the Balkan Peninsula, see: M. L. Niderle, *Manuel de l'antiquite Slave*, I–II (Paris: 1923–1926); M. Grbich, *Slovenske Starine* (Novi Sad: 1955); K. Jirecek, *Istorija Srba*, trans. J. Radonjich (Belgrade: 1952); S. Stanojevich, *Vizantija i Srbi* (Novi Sad: 1903); *Istorija Naroda Jugoslavije* (Belgrade: 1953), pp. 63–104; Konstantin VII Perfirogenit, "De Administrando Imperio," trans. N. Tomashich, *Vjesnik Hrvatsko-Slavonsko-Dalmatinskoga Zemaljskog Arhiva*, XX (1918), pp. 23–91.

A selected bibliography on the early Croatian state: Franjo Racki, *Document Historiae Croaticae Periodum Antiquam Illustranta* (Zagreb: 1877); J. Nagy, *Monumenta Diplomatica, I, Isprave iz Doba Hrvatske Narodne Demokratije* (Zagreb: 1925); M. Konstrencic, *Nacrt Historije Hrvatske Drzave i Hrvatskoga Prava I* (Zagreb: 1956); F. Sisic, *Povijest Hrvata u Vrijeme Narodnih Vladara* (Zagreb: 1925); *Istorija Naroda Jugoslavije* (Belgrade: 1953), pp. 167–228.

1. Marx and Engel, *The Communist Manifesto* (Chicago: Regnery, 1954), p. 13.

A selected bibliography on the early Slovenian state: M. Kos, *Conversio Bagoariorum et Carantanorum* (Ljubljana: 1936); F. Kos, *Gradivo za Zgodovino Slovencev v Srednjem Veku*, I–V (Ljubljana: 1902–28); B. Grafenauer, *Ustolicavenje Koroskih Vovjvod iz Drzave Karantanskih Slovencev* (Ljubljana: 1952); M. Kos, *Zgodovina Slovencev od Naselitvo do Petnajstega Stoletja* (Ljubljana: 1955); *Istorija Naroda Jugoslavije* (Belgrade: 1953), pp. 131–136.

A selected bibliography on the early Serbian state: Konstantin VII Porfirogenit, "De Administrando Imperio"; K. Jirecek, *Istorija Srba*, trans. J. Radonjich (Belgrade: 1952); *Istorija Naroga Jugoslavije* (Belgrade: 1953), pp. 229–260. S. Stanojevich and V. Corovich, *Odabrani Izvori za Srpsku Istoriju* (Belgrade: 1921); N. Radojcich, "Drustveno i Drzavno Uredjenje kod Srba u Ranom Srednjem Veku-Prema Barskom Rodoslovu," *Glasnik Srpskog Naucnog Drustva* (Belgrade: 1935).

A selected general bibliography for the whole of Yugoslavia: A. Dragnich, "Social Structure," *Yugoslavia*, ed. R. Kerner (Berkeley: University of California Press, 1949); Dr. M. Ivsich, *Diljem Sela* (Zagreb: Narodna Knjiznica, 1934); N. Halasz, *In the Shadow of Russia* (New York: Ronald, 1959); R. Kann, *The Multinational Empire: Nationalism and National Reforms in the Hapsburg Monarchy, 1848–1918* (New York: Columbia University Press, 1950); Slobodan Jovanovich, *Svetozar Markovich* (Belgrade: Dositej Obradovich, 1903); Walter Markow, "Bemerkungen zur Sudalawischen Aufklarung," Akademic der Wissenschaffen, Berlin, Institut fur Slavistik, *Deutsche-Slawische Wechselseitigkeit in Sieben Jahrhundertan* (Berlin: Akademi-Verlag, 1956); Svetozar Markovich, *Nacela Narodne Ekonomije* (Belgrade: Napredak, 1872); Karl Marx, "Turkey," New York *Tribune* (April 7, 1857); Jovan Marjanovich, *Potsetnik iz Istorije Komunisticke Partije Jugoslavije* (Belgrade: Rad, 1953); B. Newman, *The Unknown Yugoslavia* (London: Herbert Jenkins, 1960); H. Neubacher, *Sonderauftrag Sudost 1940–1945; Bericht Eines Fliegended Diplomaten* (Gottingen: Musterschmidt-Verlag, 1956), pp. 17–18; J. Skerlich, *Svetozar Markovich* (Belgrade: Napredak, 1922); R. Seton Watson, "Serbia," *Encyclopaedia Britannica*, 14th ed., XX; R. Seton Watson, *The Rise of Nationality in the Balkans* (London: Constable, 1947); R. Seton Watson, *The East European Revolution* (London: Methuen, 1950); H. Wendell, "Marxism and the Southern Slavs," *The Slavonic Review* (December 1923); United States Congress, Senate, Committee of the Judiciary, Internal Security Subcommittee, *Yugoslav Communism, A Critical Study*, prepared by Charles Zalar (Washington: Government Printing Office, 1961); *Yugoslavia* (New York: Praeger, 1957); Savez Komunista Srbije, *Materijali Sa Treceg Kongresa* (Belgrade: Rad, 1954).

I contend that the readings listed above indicate that the history of the southern Slavs has not been the history of class struggle – rather, that social thought and social movements before 1918 were either under the influence of non-Marxian Russian socialism or (as in Slovenia and Croatia) reflected struggle for national independence, and that the Communist Party in interwar Yugoslavia was a small group of dedicated believers, not a major party representing the vast majority of the Yugoslav population.

With respect to the second of the two criteria in Appendix I, the following literature shows the relation between actual economic conditions and development in the prewar Yugoslavia and the economic stagnation expected to be present – according to the second criteria – on the eve of the socialist revolution: S. Kukoleca, *Industrija Jugoslavije* (Novi Sad: Balkansra Stampa, 1940), p. 74; Dr. Bozidar Jurkovich, *Das Auslaendische Kapital in Yugoslavia* (Stuttgard, w. Kohlhammer: 1941) – this book shows that 51.39 per cent of the capital stock in 1939 belonged to foreign investors; Zagoroff, Vogh, Bilimovich, *The Agricultural Economy of Danubian Countries* (Stanford: Stanford University Press, 1955), especially p. 299; National Bank of the Kingdom of Yugoslavia, *Quarterly Bulletin* (Belgrade: October–December, issues 1928–38).

The evidence suggests that the increase in unemployment and the relatively small decrease in the rate of investment in the period 1931–41 *cannot be explained* by reasons voiced by Marx, i.e., by an increase in the ratio of capital to labor and the accelerated concentration of capital.

# *Appendix III. SOME IMPORTANT FEATURES OF THE THEORY OF ECONOMIC DEVELOPMENT OF JOSEPH SCHUMPETER*

SCHUMPETER'S point of departure is the circular flow of economic life. He believed that the only correct approach to the problem of economic changes is from a model which does not change as it flows through time.

Schumpeter constructed this model of the circular flow for a closed exchange economy in which "sellers of all the commodities appear as buyers to acquire the goods which will maintain their consumption and also productive capacity in the next period at the existing level. This does not mean that there is no change in economic activity. The data may change, but people will at once adapt to these changes and cling as tightly as possible to their habitual economic method. Thus, the economic system will not change of its own, but will be related to the preceding economic activities."[1]

The circular flow of economic life of Schumpeter has several important properties:

1. *Tradition.* Schumpeter stressed the importance of experience and long-established habits in the circular flow of economic life. They provide the entrepreneur with advance knowledge about the method of production to be used and the strength of demand for his output. "No cobbler's apprentice can repair a shoe without making some resolutions and without deciding independently some questions, however small. The 'what' and 'how' are taught him; but it does not relieve him of the necessity of a certain indifference. When a worker from an electrical firm goes into a house to repair the lighting system, even he must decide something of the what and how. . . . But the what and the how are also taught him . . . given circumstances force him to act in a definite way. . . . people who direct business firms only execute what is prescribed for them by wants and demand and by the given means and method of production."[2]

1. M. Sh. Khan, *Schumpeter's Theory of Capitalist Development* (India: Muslim University, 1957), p. 2.

2. Schumpeter, *The Theory of Economic Development* (Cambridge: Harvard Economic Studies, 1959), pp. 20–21.

2. *Factors of Production.* Schumpeter, like his teacher Böhm-Bawerk, recognized only two productive agents: labor and land. He said that "we can resolve all goods into labor and land in the sense that we can conceive of all goods as bundles of the services of labor and land."[3] For Schumpeter, the entrepreneur is not a factor of production whose contribution to the output can be calculated by using marginal analysis, but the entrepreneur is the motor of economic development. On the other hand, Schumpeter defines "capital" as "a fund of purchasing power."[4] According to Schumpeter, capital has *only one* function: "Capital is nothing but the lever by which the entrepreneur subjects to his control the concrete goods which he needs, nothing but a means of diverting the factors of production to new uses, or of dictating a new direction to production."[5] Hence, in the circular flow of economic life capital does not perform a function – i.e., there is no capital in a model without development.

3. *Pricing in the Circular Flow of Economic Life.* Marginal analysis explains price determination. Assuming competition in the model, the value of the national output will eventually be distributed among labor and land. Therefore, profits are zero in the circular flow of economic life.

4. *Production Function.* In the circular flow of economic life the production function is constant, i.e., the index of significance of input relative to output does not change. Therefore, only quantitative variations are possible as inputs are substituted one for another at the margin, and the system yields deterministic solutions.

To explain the mechanism of economic development, Schumpeter injected into the circular flow of economic life both entrepreneurship and changing production function and related them in such a way that it is the entrepreneur who brings about a change in production function and breaks up the circular flow. The act of changing the production function Schumpeter called "innovation." Capital appears here in the form of *power*, needed to divert resources from their previous uses. Innovating action calls for a change in the index of significance of inputs relative to output; hence, the process of economic development includes, by definition, both quantitative (substitution at the margin) and qualitative (change in production function) variations. In summary, the scope and the timing of innovating actions are not predictable, but the government and other responsible institutions can influence the rate of economic development by creating an environment conducive to the exercise of entrepreneurial decisions. Thus, the problem of development appears to be primarily the problem of finding the right organization.

3. *Ibid.*, p. 17.
4. *Ibid.*, p. 120.
5. *Ibid.*, p. 116.

# *Appendix IV. FOREIGN TRADE, TANGIBLE FOREIGN AID, AND LOANS FROM THE INTERNATIONAL BANK*

THE data for Appendix Tables 1–4 were taken from the *Statistical Pocketbook of Yugoslavia*, 1962, p. 69; *ibid.*, 1963, pp. 66–68; and *Statisticki Godisnjak*, 1964, p. 224. The data for Appendix Table 5 were taken from *U.S. Foreign Assistance, July 1, 1945–June 30, 1961* (rev.; Washington, D.C.: Agency for International Development, 1962), p. 25. The data for Appendix Table 6 were taken from the *1961–1962 Seventeenth Annual Report* published by the International Bank for Reconstruction and Development (Washington, D.C., 1962), p. 67.

Appendix Table 1. Balance of Trade

| Year | Exports [a] | Imports [a] | Balance [a] | Exports/ Imports [b] |
|---|---|---|---|---|
| 1939 ...... | 5,521 | 4,757 | + 764 | 116 |
| 1955 ...... | 76,976 | 98,092 [c] | −21,116 | 78 |
| 1956 ...... | 97,011 | 111,680 [c] | −14,669 | 87 |
| 1957 ...... | 118,533 | 162,536 [c] | −44,003 | 73 |
| 1958 ...... | 132,419 | 180,403 [c] | −47,984 | 73 |
| 1959 ...... | 142,995 | 174,884 [c] | −31,889 | 82 |
| 1960 ...... | 169,848 | 229,466 [c] | −59,618 | 74 |
| 1961 ...... | 170,670 | 247,152 [c] | −76,482 | 69 |
| 1962 ...... | 207,146 | 237,225 [c] | −30,079 | 87 |
| 1963[d] ..... | 237,103 | 282,586 [c] | −45,483 | 84 |

[a] In millions of dinars.

[b] As percentage.

[c] The data for 1955–63 exclude the economic aid and agricultural surpluses imports from the United States, which amounted to 34,196 million dinars in 1955, 32,048 million in 1956, 35,858 million in 1957, 25,101 million in 1958, 31,272 million in 1959, 18,450 million in 1960, 25,935 million in 1961, 29,092 million in 1962, and 34,400 million in 1963.

[d] January through September.

Appendix Table 2. Exports and Imports by Commodity Sections (in Millions of Dinars)

| Commodity Sections | 1958 | 1960 | 1962 |
|---|---|---|---|
| *Exports* | | | |
| Food | 40,258 | 48,176 | 48,276 |
| Beverages and tobacco | 11,321 | 7,961 | 8,950 |
| Crude materials, inedible | 2,446 | 26,550 | 28,679 |
| Mineral fuels and lubricants | 1,742 | 1,548 | 5,270 |
| Oils and fats, technical | 8 | 394 | 201 |
| Chemicals | 4,377 | 6,901 | 6,451 |
| Manufactured goods [a] | 30,595 | 40,203 | 46,885 |
| Machinery and transport equipment | 14,124 | 25,398 | 47,303 |
| Manufactured articles | 7,337 | 11,490 | 15,176 |
| Miscellaneous | 211 | 1,227 | 176 |
| Total | 132,419 | 169,848 | 207,317 |
| *Imports* | | | |
| Food | 39,160 | 22,659 | 38,008 |
| Beverages and tobacco | 337 | 21 | 1,164 |
| Crude materials, inedible | 25,226 | 35,516 | 39,849 |
| Mineral fuels and lubricants | 12,368 | 13,505 | 39,849 |
| Oils and fats, technical | 4,311 | 3,456 | 14,403 |
| Chemicals | 20,030 | 21,418 | 4,288 |
| Manufactured goods [a] | 32,473 | 51,527 | 48,890 |
| Machinery and transport equipment | 64,703 | 91,338 | 87,933 |
| Manufactured articles | 6,088 | 8,145 | 8,402 |
| Miscellaneous | 808 | 331 | 119 |
| Total | 205,504 | 247,916 | 266,427 |

[a] Classified chiefly by material.

Appendix Table 3. Exports and Imports by Principal Countries (in Millions of Dinars)

| Principal Countries | Exports | | Imports | |
|---|---|---|---|---|
| | 1960 | 1961 | 1960 | 1961 |
| Europe | 131,603 | 127,362 | 182,595 | 186,081 |
| Austria | 9,025 | 7,629 | 11,231 | 9,765 |
| Belgium | 1,383 | 1,256 | 2,632 | 4,110 |
| Czechoslovakia | 7,713 | 4,876 | 7,927 | 5,940 |
| France | 2,631 | 2,870 | 8,301 | 6,933 |
| Greece | 5,759 | 5,900 | 2,398 | 4,375 |
| Netherlands | 1,791 | 1,574 | 4,306 | 3,554 |
| Italy | 22,544 | 20,839 | 28,488 | 39,528 |
| Hungary | 6,116 | 5,453 | 10,985 | 9,784 |
| German Dem. Rep. | 13,919 | 8,486 | 11,199 | 11,253 |
| Poland | 6,603 | 11,753 | 11,367 | 8,487 |
| Rumania | 1,792 | 3,108 | 2,689 | 2,493 |
| Fed. Rep. of Germany | 15,267 | 16,492 | 37,029 | 42,704 |
| U.S.S.R. | 15,915 | 14,188 | 17,170 | 9,593 |
| Switzerland | 2,448 | 2,176 | 5,379 | 4,547 |
| Sweden | 1,481 | 1,659 | 2,576 | 2,930 |
| United Kingdom | 13,034 | 14,550 | 13,623 | 13,734 |
| Other countries | 4,182 | 4,553 | 5,295 | 6,351 |
| Asia | 13,556 | 15,974 | 13,140 | 13,101 |
| Burma | 1,319 | 588 | 929 | 30 |
| India | 2,258 | 4,937 | 2,544 | 2,405 |
| Indonesia | 3,550 | 4,533 | 200 | 552 |
| Iraq | 478 | 401 | 407 | 1,232 |
| Israel | 1,321 | 2,292 | 1,382 | 1,688 |
| China | 348 | ... | 159 | 9 |
| Malaya | 3 | 8 | 2,369 | 2,212 |
| Pakistan | 605 | 463 | 473 | 728 |
| Turkey | 961 | 772 | 712 | 692 |
| Other countries | 2,713 | 1,980 | 3,668 | 3,553 |
| Africa | 10,219 | 8,759 | 15,653 | 6,279 |
| Algeria | 345 | 164 | 48 | 6 |
| Union of South Africa | 79 | 76 | 1,318 | 649 |
| Morocco | 196 | 184 | 911 | 674 |
| United Arab Republic | 6,378 | 5,890 | 10,776 | 2,429 |
| Other countries | 3,221 | 2,445 | 2,600 | 2,521 |
| North America | 11,866 | 12,597 | 28,072 | 55,220 |
| Canada | 222 | 330 | 925 | 328 |
| U.S.A. | 11,477 | 10,829 | 26,574 | 54,057 |
| Other countries | 167 | 1,438 | 573 | 835 |
| South America | 2,810 | 2,139 | 4,652 | 6,129 |
| Argentina | 592 | 1,267 | 1,610 | 3,056 |
| Brazil | 1,712 | 568 | 2,008 | 2,292 |
| Uruguay | 234 | 127 | 420 | 372 |
| Other countries | 272 | 177 | 614 | 409 |
| Oceania | 26 | 30 | 4,083 | 3,513 |
| Total | 170,080 | 166,861 | 248,195 | 270,323 |

Appendix Table 4. Exports and Imports by Stage of Production (in Percentage)

| Stage of Production | Exports | | | | | Imports | | | | |
|---|---|---|---|---|---|---|---|---|---|---|
| | 1939 | 1959 | 1960 | 1961 | 1962 | 1939 | 1959 | 1960 | 1961 | 1962 |
| Crude | 56 | 26 | 26 | 25 | 19 | 20 | 30 | 20 | 24 | 27 |
| Semi-manufactured | 39 | 37 | 39 | 38 | 38 | 26 | 23 | 23 | 22 | 22 |
| Manufactured | 5 | 37 | 35 | 37 | 43 | 54 | 47 | 57 | 54 | 51 |

Appendix Table 5. United States Foreign Aid to Yugoslavia, 1946–61 (in Millions of Dollars)

| Year | Grants | Loans | Total Economic Aid |
|---|---|---|---|
| 1946–48 | 298.1 | ... | 298.1 |
| 1949 | ... | ... | ... |
| 1950 | ... | 40.0 | 40.0 |
| 1951 | 80.5 | 15.0 | 95.5 |
| 1952 | 106.3 | ... | 106.3 |
| 1953 | 122.6 | ... | 122.6 |
| 1954 | 67.6 | ... | 67.6 |
| 1955 | 143.4 | ... | 143.4 |
| 1956 | 74.2 | 24.0 | 98.2 |
| 1957 | 34.3 | 88.0 | 122.3 |
| 1958 | 35.5 | 60.6 | 96.1 |
| 1959 | 46.3 | 128.4 | 174.7 |
| 1960 | 26.7 | 49.4 | 76.1 |
| 1961 | 31.6 | 116.4 | 148.0 |
| Total | 1,064.2 | 521.8 | 1,586.0 |

Appendix Table 6. Loans from the International Bank for Reconstruction and Development

| Date | Amount [a] | Interest Rate |
|---|---|---|
| 1951 | 28,000,000 | 4½ |
| 1953 | 30,000,000 | 4⅞ |
| 1961 | 30,000,000 | 5¾ |
| Total | 88,000,000 | |

[a] In United States dollars.

# *Appendix V. WORKERS' MANAGEMENT OF A FIRM IN YUGOSLAVIA*

THIS appendix quotes a few original decisions made by Workers' Councils and Executive Boards in Yugoslavia, the content of which should help to understand better the scope and nature of the rights and duties of the workers in Yugoslavia.

Unfortunately, I have records from only one firm in Yugoslavia and for this reason cannot generalize from the example. It can serve only as a remote indication of what might be the scope of rights and duties of the Workers' Council and Executive Board in Yugoslavia.

The firm is Rade Koncar of Zagreb, Croatia – one of the largest enterprises in Yugoslavia, employing about 3,800 employees in 1957. The enterprise produces hydroelectric and turbo generators, small and medium-sized electric motors, transformers, electrical traction equipment, and so forth. To illustrate the decisions of a meeting of the Workers' Council, I quote the decisions of the second regular meeting of the Workers' Council held on May 17, 1957:

"1. The Workers' Council has elected two delegates to the first Congress of the Workers' Councils of Yugoslavia, Branko Pocekaj and Ing. Ante Markovic.

"They are instructed to prepare materials to submit to the Congress by June 10, which they shall previously examine with the Workers' Council.

"2. The Workers' Council, after discussion, has approved the report of the transfer of office between the former Managing Board and the newly elected Managing Board. The transfer report is attached to the minutes.

"3. With reference to the proposal made by the Managing Board, the Workers' Council approves distribution of the monies of the Fund for Independent Disposal of 1956 as follows (in dinars):

| | |
|---|---|
| Total Fund for Independent Disposal, according to the financial Balance Sheet for 1956 .......................... | 13,645,654 |

| | | |
|---|---|---|
| Released part of the pledges for 1956 credited the Fund by National Bank........ | 11,750,040 | |
| Projected Requirements in 1957: | | |
| Deposit of 10% of estimates for construction of apartment building in Veslacka Street .......................... | 5,200,000 | |
| Deposit of 10% of sum for continued construction in Voltino Naselje apartments.. | 5,000,000 | |
| Annuity due to City Savings Bank for building in Bojnovic Street ............... | 7,125,200 | |
| Business relations expenses ............. | 2,000,000 | |
| Other permanent expenses.............. | 250,000 | |
| Awards to efficiency experts and inventors.. | 1,000,000 | |
| 10% of estimated advertisement expenses.. | 2,052,000 | |
| Expenditures for anti-aircraft defense..... | 600,000 | |
| Membership fees in associations and organizations ........................... | 200,000 | |
| Grants to social organizations........... | 6,500,000 | |
| Publication of six issues of *Vjesnik* [bimonthly newsletter of plant].......... | 1,890,000 | |
| Subsidy for heating factory restaurant ..... | 400,000 | |
| Installations for removing metal splinters from eyes ......................... | 103,000 | |
| Linoleum for first-aid station ........... | 192,000 | |
| Balance (deficit) ................... | | 7,116,503 |

"The Workers' Council approves that the deficit should be compensated by successively deducting from the Pay Fund the amount of 4,700,000 dinars and by transferring it to the Fund for Independent Disposal to make good the difference of 7,116,503 dinars.

"4. The Workers' Council charges the Commission for Personnel to propose a draft program for a workers' management seminar in five days' time.

Chairman of the Workers' Council
(signed) Zvonimir Vinko"[1]

To illustrate the decisions of the Executive Board, I quote a few decisions adopted at the thirtieth regular meeting of the Board (December 30, 1957):

"The Managing Board approves a trip of fifteen days for Vladimir Bogatec and Vladimir Tadejovic, for nine days in Czechoslovakia, five days in Austria, and one day in West Germany for the purpose of purchasing raw materials. Travel expenses and personal allowances are to

1. M. Bogosavljevich and M. Pesakovich, *Workers' Management of a Factory in Yugoslavia* (Belgrade: Yugoslavia, 1959), pp. 34–35.

be charged against our enterprise according to the specification attached to the minutes, totaling 221,958 dinars, the Managing Board approving deduction against personal allowances by 20 per cent and special hotel expenses.

"The Managing Board has decided that the third advance against the surplus of the Pay Fund amounting to 20 per cent of one month's salaries be paid to all workers and office employees on December 27, 1957. Persons to whom Point 2 of the Decisions of the third regular meeting of the Workers' Council held on May 24, 1957, pertains, who received more than their due as pay according to the Pay Scale, will receive their advances diminished by the amount received in excess, but only up to 50 per cent of the advance being paid.

"The Managing Board has decided to pay all the workers and office employees of our restaurant a sum equal to 50 per cent of one month's pay as a New Year's Bonus.

"The Managing Board has decided to propose to the Workers' Council to grant the Council of the Producers of the Peoples' Committee of the City of Zagreb the sum of 500,000 dinars as a contribution from our plant for the construction of the 'Mosa Pijade' Workers' University in Zagreb."[2]

2. *Ibid.*, p. 38.

# *Appendix VI. PUBLIC ANNOUNCEMENTS*

THIS appendix offers a few examples of public announcements with respect to the procedure for the appointment of the director of a firm, allocation of investment funds, and liquidation of a Yugoslav firm:

"*The commission for the appointment of directors of enterprises, borough Zvezdara, Belgrade*, announces the contest for the director of the firm *Gradska Cistoca* in Belgrade.

"Requirements: B.A. or similar degree and experience in communal problems. Applications, including fifty dinars in tax stamps, diploma, detailed biography, and proof that the applicant has no criminal record should be sent to the borough Zvezdara, Belgrade, not later than fifteen days from the date."[1]

"*XLVII contest for Investment Loans from the G.I.F. for Construction, Expansion and Modernization of Black Metallurgy*. The Yugoslav Investment Bank will give . . . credits for ore mining; production of steel; production of iron; production of steel cables; production of coke; production of inflammable materials needed for production of iron. . . . Requirements: that the objects built will be finished by the end of 1963; that the investor will participate in financing the project; that the amount of loan, including 4 per cent interest a year, will be paid in less than thirty years. . . . Preferential consideration will be given to the investors who: have the lowest cost of production, have the largest rate of profit, will increase supply of the products in strong demand, offer the largest participation in financing their respective projects, and propose to repay loans in the shortest period of time. . . . The investors are invited to submit their applications for loans including the analysis of projects ninety days from the date."[2]

"*The compulsory liquidation of the firm Partizan from Lajkovac, Serbia*. The court in Belgrade has started the process of compulsory liq-

1. Yugoslavia, *Sluzbeni List* (Belgrade: April 18, 1962), p. III.
2. Yugoslavia, *Sluzbeni List* (Belgrade: January 7, 1962), p. 610.

uidation of the firm *Partizan* from Lajkovac. The judge in charge of the liquidation is Ljubisa Milic and the executor Jovanovich Dusan from Lajkovac. All creditors are invited to submit their claims to the court in Belgrade within thirty days." [3]

"*The Regular Liquidation of the restaurant Split, in Ljubljana.* Restaurant *Split*, Ljubljana, Vidovdanaka Street, No. 1 has been ordered in the regular liquidation by the local government of Ljubljana." [4]

3. Yugoslavia, *Sluzbeni List* (Belgrade: April 18, 1962), p. I.
4. Yugoslavia, *Sluzbeni List* (Belgrade: April 19, 1962), p. I.

# Notes

# NOTES

## *Chapter I. The Legal Structure of the Yugoslav Economy, pages 3–36*

1. Yugoslavia, *Sluzbeni List* (*Official Bulletin*). Belgrade: June 12, 1945, Pravni Akt (Legislative Act) 359. Subsequent citations of this kind will be given as: *SL*, June 12, 1945, PA 359.
2. *SL*, July 13, 1946, PA 432.
3. *SL*, April 4, 1947, PA 209.
4. *SL*, September 6, 1948, PA 732.
5. *SL*, December 6, 1946, PA 677.
6. *SL*, April 28, 1948, PA 269.
7. *SL*, December 31, 1958, PA 890.
8. *SL*, June 9, 1949, PA 412.
9. *SL*, January 29, 1954, PA 48.
10. *SL*, February 6, 1963, PA 63.
11. Robert F. Byrnes, ed., *Yugoslavia* (New York: Praeger, 1957), p. 228.
12. *SL*, August 28, 1945, PA 605.
13. *SL*, May 27, 1953, PA 150.
14. Jozo Tomasevich, *Peasants, Politics, and Economic Change in Yugoslavia* (Stanford: Stanford University Press, 1955), p. 384. The second agrarian reform affected only 66,459 out of more than 2,000,000 private holdings. See *The Yugoslav Survey* (Belgrade: Yugoslavia Publishing House, 1961), p. 791.
15. *SL*, July 23, 1946, PA 412.
16. *SL*, June 9, 1949, PA 411.
17. V. Jagich, *Historija Knjizevnosti Naroda Hrvatskog i Srpskog* (Zagreb: Dragutin Albrecht, 1867), p. 15 (my translation).
18. J. La Farge, S.J., *Martyrdom of Slovenia* (New York: American Press, 1942), p. 1.
19. *SL*, November 20, 1945, PA 854.
20. *SL*, August 21, 1948, PA 596.
21. *SL*, March 30, 1953, PA 83.
22. *SL*, August 23, 1946, PA 484.
23. *SL*, April 7, 1954, PA 170.
24. G. W. Hoffman and F. W. Neal, *Yugoslavia and the New Communism* (New York: Twentieth Century Fund, 1962), p. 288.
25. *Statisticki Godisnjak*, 1964, pp. 142, 156, and 164.
26. *SL*, June 4, 1946, PA 302.
27. *SL*, May 15, 1945, PA 282.
28. *SL*, June 3, 1947, PA 360.
29. *SL*, December 30, 1951, PA 569.

30. *SL*, December 31, 1953, PA 485.

31. D. Rajilich, "U Cemu je Monopolizam Jedinstvene Banke," *Glasnik Narodne Banke* (Belgrade: November 1953), pp. 6–7; M. Ugricich, "Banke u Novom Privrednon Sistemu," *Glasnik Narodne Banke* (Belgrade: January–February 1954), pp. 1–5.

32. R. Jankovich *et al.*, eds., *Zbirka Propisa o Bankarstvu i o Poslovanju sa Bankom* (Belgrade: Nova Administracija, 1957), pp. 9–29.

33. *Ibid.*

34. Milos Vuckovich, "The Recent Development of the Money and Banking System of Yugoslavia," *Journal of Political Economy*, August 1963, p. 374.

35. There are three specialized banks in Yugoslavia. The Yugoslav Bank for Foreign Trade was founded June 29, 1955, the Yugoslav Investment Bank July 18, 1956, and the Yugoslav Agricultural Bank June 27, 1958.

36. *SL*, March 15, 1961, PA 118.

37. *SL*, January 31, 1954, PA 30.

38. Jankovich, pp. 77–90.

39. *Ibid.*, pp. 106–110.

40. "Zakoni o Bankama i o Kreditnim i Drugim Poslovima" (Belgrade: *Sluzbeni List*, 1961), pp. 88, 93–95, 98.

41. *SL*, March 27, 1955, PA 94 and 95.

42. Jankovich, pp. 44–47.

43. *Ibid.*, p. 47.

44. *SL*, April 5, 1961, PA 213.

45. See, for example, Ludwig Von Mises, *Planned Chaos* (New York: Foundation for Economic Education, 1947); Friedrich A. Hayek, *The Road to Serfdom* (Chicago: University of Chicago Press, 1944).

46. See Hans Hirsch, *Quantity Planning and Price Planning in the Soviet Union* (Philadelphia: University of Pennsylvania Press, 1961).

47. See in particular Oskar Lange and Fred Taylor, *On the Economic Theory of Socialism* (Minneapolis: University of Minnesota Press, 1938), and Maurice Dobb, *Essay on Economic Growth and Planning* (New York: Monthly Review Press, 1960), Ch. VI.

48. Lange and Taylor, pp. 92–93.

49. *Ibid.*, p. 93.

50. *SL*, January 17, 1951, PA 59.

51. *SL*, May 30, 1951, PA 265.

52. *SL*, September 5, 1951, PA 387.

53. *SL*, June 18, 1952, PA 382.

54. *SL*, August 17, 1955, PA 430.

55. *Zbirka Propisa iz Oblasti Cena* (Belgrade: Zajednica, 1965).

56. M. Spiljak, *System of Remuneration in Yugoslavia* (Belgrade: Yugoslav Publishing House, 1961), p. 14.

57. Franklyn D. Holzman, *Soviet Taxation* (Cambridge: Harvard University Press, 1955), p. 68.

58. *SL*, July 5, 1950, PA 391.

59. *SL*, December 26, 1953, PA 433. The provisions of this act were reaffirmed in the new constitution of 1963, Article IX, paragraph 3: ". . . The employees of the enterprise divide, either directly or by way of their respective Workers' Councils, about the use of means of production and their disposal, and see that the means of production are economically employed so that the maximum results are obtained for society as well as for the firm." See *Prednacrt Ustava Federativne Socijalisticke Republike Jugoslavije*, p. 12.

60. *SL*, December 24, 1953, PA 422.

61. Jankovich, pp. 243–277.

62. *SL*, March 2, 1961, PA 59; *SL*, March 2, 1961, PA 64; *SL*, April 12, 1961,

PA 236. The last act determined the guaranteed minimum wage for each industry. Fifteen months later a minimum wage of 9,600 dinars a month was decreed (see *Politika*, July 1, 1962).

63. *SL*, April 18, 1962, PA 210.
64. *SL*, August 2, 1946, PA 437.
65. *SL*, January 30, 1952, PA 49.
66. *SL*, December 24, 1953, PA 424.
67. *Politika*, July 22, 1962.
68. *SL*, December 26, 1951, PA 545.
69. *SL*, December 24, 1953, PA 425.
70. *SL*, October 2, 1948, PA 711.
71. *Zakon o Radnim Odnosima* (Belgrade: *Sluzbeni List*, 1958).
72. *SL*, December 15, 1948, PA 883.
73. *SL*, June 7, 1961, PA 377.

## *Chapter II. Economic Planning in Yugoslavia, pages 37–57*

1. Milton Friedman, "Money and Business Cycles," unpublished paper, April 4, 1962.
2. Arnold Haberger, "The Incidence of the Corporate Income Tax," *Journal of Political Economy*, June 1962, pp. 215–240.
3. Two very good works on Soviet economic planning are Nicholas Spulber, *The Soviet Economy* (New York: Norton, 1962), and H. Levine, "The Central Planning of Supply in Soviet Industry," in Joint Economic Committee, *Comparison of the United States and Soviet Economies* (Washington: Government Printing Office, 1959).
4. Stojan Novakovich, "Plan Narodne Privrede kao Sredstvo Ekonomske Politike," in Stojan Novakovich *et al.*, eds., *Ekonomska Politika* (Belgrade: 1959), pp. 73–104.
5. *The Law on the Five Year Plan . . .* (Belgrade: Government Office of Information, 1947).
6. *The Social Plan for 1962* (Belgrade, January 1962). This is an unofficial translation, prepared by a translator who is not an economist for the use of the United States Embassy in Belgrade.
7. See Tibor Scitovsky, *Welfare and Competition* (Chicago: Irwin, 1951), p. 174.
8. For theoretical analysis of the importance of marginal contributions from outside see Celso Furtado, "Capital Formation and Economic Development," in *The Economics of Underdevelopment*, A. N. Agarwala and S. P. Singh, eds. (London: Oxford University Press, 1958), pp. 309–337.
9. See Maurice Dobb, *Essay on Economic Growth and Planning* (New York: Monthly Review Press, 1960), p. 29.
10. In this context may be mentioned Professor William Baumol's exciting and somewhat radical plan of tax rebates. See Klaus Knorr and William Baumol, *What Price Economic Growth?* (Englewood Cliffs, N.J.: Prentice-Hall, 1961), pp. 30–47.
11. United Nations, *Economic Survey of Europe, 1959* (Geneva: United Nations, 1961).
12. *Social Plan, 1957–1961* (Belgrade: *Sluzbeni List*, 1957), and *Economic Development with Stability, A Report to the Government of India* (International Monetary Fund: 1953), p. 19.

## *Chapter III. The Performance of the Yugoslav Economy, pages 58–84*

1. *Statistical Pocketbook of Yugoslavia* (Belgrade: Federal Statistical Institute, 1961), p. 153.

2. *Ibid.*, p. 154. Some elements of double-counting seem to be present in the Yugoslav statistics.
3. "Subjektivizam u Koncepciji Drustvenog Proizvoda," *Ekonomski Pregled*, No. 6, 1965, pp. 381–403.
4. *Ibid.*
5. *Economska Politika* (Belgrade), February 2, 1957, p. 8.
6. There is plenty of evidence today concerning the scope and extent of black market activities in the U.S.S.R. See H. Levine, "The Central Planning of Supply in Soviet Industry," Part I, and also David Granick, *The Red Executive* (New York: Doubleday, 1960), among other works.
7. See his view of the double law of degeneration and revitalization of energy, in Jacques Maritain, *The Rights of Man and Natural Law* (New York: Scribner, 1951), p. 30.
8. New York *Times*, December 17, 1963, p. 10.
9. M. Vuckovich, "The Recent Development of the Money and Banking System of Yugoslavia," *Journal of Political Economy*, August 1963, p. 368.
10. *Borba*, April 22, 1962, p. 4.
11. New York *Times*, December 17, 1963, p. 10.
12. Vuckovich, p. 368.
13. *Ibid.*, p. 363.
14. Quoted in Charles P. McVicker, *Titoism* (New York: St. Martin's, 1957), p. 61.
15. Oskar Lange and Fred Taylor, *On The Economic Theory of Socialism* (Minneapolis: University of Minnesota Press, 1938), pp. 72–78.
16. Branko Horvat, "Optimum Rate of Investment," *Economic Journal*, December 1958, pp. 747–767.
17. Djordje Misich, "Investicije i Njihovo Koriscenje kao Sredstava Ekonomske Politike," in Stojan Novakovich *et al.*, eds., *Ekonomska Politika* (Belgrade, 1959), pp. 105–117. Professor Misich's analysis of the upper and lower limits of investment concurs with the analysis in Chapter II of the present volume, although he uses different terminology.
18. *Statisticki Godisnjak*, 1962, p. 97; and also the *Statistical Pocketbook*, 1965, p. 40.
19. E. Neuberger, "The Yugoslav Investment Auction," *Quarterly Journal of Economics*, February 1959, pp. 88–115.
20. *Economic Survey of Europe, 1959* (New York: United Nations, 1960), pp. 34–45.
21. This also seems to be confirmed by F. Vasic in "The Yugoslav System of Investment Financing and the Application of Criteria in the Selection of Investment Projects," *Engineering Economics*, Fall 1960, pp. 1–8.
22. *Politika*, July 22, 1962.
23. Theodore Schultz, "Investment in Human Capital," *American Economic Review*, March 1961, pp. 1–17.
24. Cyril Zebot, *Economics of Competitive Coexistence* (New York: Praeger, 1964).
25. M. Markovich, *Uvod u Ekonomiku Jugoslavije* (Zagreb: Naprijed, 1959), p. 109.
26. *Borba*, March 8, 1962.
27. See J. W. Kendrick, *Productivity Trends in the United States* (Princeton: Princeton University Press, 1961).
28. *Statisticki Godisnjak*, 1961, p. 236.
29. *Three-Monthly Bulletin of Yugoslavia*, July 1960, p. 1.
30. "Tito's Economic Difficulties," New York *Times*, March 27, 1962.

## *Chapter IV. The Firm in Yugoslavia, pages 85–104*

1. *Borba*, March 2, 1962.
2. "Zakon o Kreditima i Drugim Bankarskim Poslovima," *Zakoni o Bankama* (Belgrade: *Sluzbeni List*, 1961), pp. 65–71.
3. Djordje Peklich, "Novi Kreditni i Bankarski Sistem," *Narodna Uprava* (Sarajevo), September 1961, pp. 90–98.
4. Benjamin Ward, "Workers' Management in Yugoslavia," *Journal of Political Economy*, October 1957, pp. 373–386; and comment by Branko Horvat and V. Roskovich, *ibid.*, April 1959, pp. 194–199.
5. Benjamin Ward, "The Firm in Illyria: Market Syndicalism," *American Economic Review*, September 1958, p. 570.
6. John T. Dunlop, *Industrial Relations Systems* (New York: Holt, Rinehart, and Winston, 1959), Ch. VII, especially pp. 294–296.
7. Svetozar Pejovich, "Yugoslavia Today," *Problems of Communism*, September–October 1962, p. 64.
8. *Politika*, July 24, 1962.
9. New York *Times*, August 3, 1962, p. 3.
10. *Politika*, July 21, 1962.
11. See M. Dautovich, *Ekonomika i Organizacija Preduzeca* (Belgrade: Savremena Administracije, 1959), pp. 84–97.
12. Djordje Misich, "Dalja Razrada Privrednog Sistema," *Nova Administracija*, February 1961, pp. 105–114.
13. *Ibid.*, p. 111.
14. Milos Vuckovich, "Promjene u Sistemu Raspodele Ukupnog Prihoda i Dohotka Privrednih Organizacija" in *Narodna Uprava* for March and April 1961, pp. 81–90.
15. S. Novakovich, "Sistem i Politika Cena u Nasoj Privredi," in S. Novakovich *et al.*, eds., *Ekonomska Politika* (Belgrade: 1959), pp. 117–144.
16. *Politika*, February 28, 1962.

## *Chapter V. Analytical Explanation of the Performance of the Yugoslav Economy, pages 105–119*

1. Goetz Briefs, "The Ethos Problem in the Present Pluralistic Society," *Review of Social Economy*, March 1957, pp. 47–75.
2. Asa Briggs, "The Language of Class in the Early Nineteenth Century," *Essays in Labor History* (London: Macmillan, 1960), p. 67.
3. See *Mater et Magistra* and also Goetz Briefs, "Cartels, Realism or Escapism," *Review of Politics*, January 1946, pp. 68–94.
4. William Fellner, *Modern Economic Analysis* (New York: McGraw-Hill, 1960), pp. 221–225.
5. In the text I refer to their respective works as Chamberlin's theory of monopolistic competition.
6. This was the point made by Schumpeter. See Joseph Schumpeter, *Business Cycles* (New York: McGraw-Hill, 1939), pp. 56–68. Chamberlin challenged Schumpeter's analysis in *Towards a More General Theory of Value* (New York: Oxford University Press, 1954), pp. 215–226.
7. John M. Keynes, *The General Theory of Employment, Interest and Money* (New York: Harcourt, Brace and World, 1936).
8. See John R. Hicks, *A Contribution to the Theory of the Trade Cycle* (London: Oxford University Press, 1961).
9. William Baumol, *Economic Dynamics* (New York: Macmillan, 1951), p. 35.
10. John M. Clark, "Realism and Relevance in the Theory of Demand," *Journal of Political Economy*, August 1946, pp. 347–353.

11. John K. Galbraith, *The Affluent Society* (Boston: Houghton Mifflin, 1958), Ch. II.

12. Cyril Zebot, "Economics of Affluence," *Review of Social Economy*, September 1959, pp. 112–125.

13. Joseph Schumpeter, *The Theory of Economic Development* (Cambridge: Harvard University Press, 1959), p. 65.

14. Joseph Schumpeter, preface to the Japanese edition of *The Theory of Economic Development.*

15. See John K. Galbraith, *The Journey to Poland and Yugoslavia* (Cambridge: Harvard University Press, 1958), appendix on economic power.

16. Joseph Solterer, "Quadragesimo Anno, Schumpeter's Alternative to the Omnipotent State," *Review of Social Economy*, March 1951, pp. 12–23.

17. See Joseph Solterer, "La Naturaliza del Poder Economico," in *Direcciones Contemporares del Pensamienta Economico*, ed. E. E. Borga (La Plata: 1961).

18. Two suggestions for the organization of the economy along these lines are found in Neyman's concept of dynamic indeterminism, for which see Joseph Neyman, "Indeterminism in Science and New Demands on Statisticians," *Journal of the American Statistical Association*, January 1961, pp. 1–10, and Solterer's concept of "steady state" in his "Structure of a Pluralistic Economy," *Review of Social Economy*, March 1956, pp. 1–26.

19. Tito's speech at the Fifth Congress of S.S.N.R.J. on March 10, 1960.

20. Jovan Djordjevich, "Teorija o Birokratiji," *Arhiv* (Belgrade: July 1960), pp. 207–238.

21. Radivoje Uvalich, "O Odnosima u Proizvodnji," *Problemi Politicke Ekonomije Socijalizma*, ed. R. Stojanovich (Belgrade: Rad, 1958), pp. 89–98.

22. Djordje Peklich, "Novi Kreditni i Bankarski Sistem," *Narodna Uprava* (Sarajevo: September 1961), pp. 90–98.

23. Nikola Vuckovich, "Uloge Credita in Nasoj Privredi," *Ekonomska Politika Jugoslavija*, ed. D. Todorovich (Belgrade: Rad, 1957), pp. 234–270.

# Index

# *INDEX*